Gifted for Life's Journey

Why You Are Unique

Dr. Chuck McAlister

Promise of Hope Ministries
Hot Springs, Arkansas

Copyright © 2006 by Chuck McAlister.
Printed in the United States of America.

ISBN 0-9726016-1-9
Dewey Decimal Classification 234

Cover design by Zach Kennedy

Unless otherwise stated, Scripture quotations are from:
The Holy Bible, New King James Version
© 1984 by Thomas Nelson, Inc.

First printing 2006

All rights reserved.

No part of this publication may be reproduced, stored in a retrieval system, or transmitted, in any form or by any means—electronic, mechanical, photocopying, recording, or otherwise—without prior written permission from the author.

For information:
Promise of Hope Ministries
3100 East Grand Avenue
Hot Springs, Arkansas 71901

Acknowledgements

As with nearly everything I do, this book would not have happened without a host of very dedicated people.

To Bill and Pat Bledsoe, thank you for believing in what God wants to do through this book and the other projects we have undertaken together. You are the best of friends and it is a joy to serve our Lord with you. It is by your efforts that this volume has come together.

To Stephanie, my personal assistant, thank you for keeping me on track and organized. You are the best.

To the board of Promise of Hope Ministries, Sherrill Schroeder, Bill Bledsoe, and Russell Kennedy; your prayers have sustained me in more ways than you will ever know.

To The Church at Crossgate Center, thank you for putting up with a pastor who is always stretching you, and thank you for stretching me. Your willingness to continually launch me out to engage in ministry has been a tremendous blessing in my life. It is a privilege to be your pastor.

To my son Chris, thank you for the way you have challenged me and stretched me by the remarkable leadership skills you display. You have inspired me to be a better leader. I love learning from you. I am honored to be your Dad.

To my daughter-in-law, Brandi, thank you for the heart you have brought to our family. You are more of a blessing than you will ever know. I love you so much. You are such a joy. Thank you for teaching our granddaughters to love Jesus like you do.

To my son Jeff, follow the vision God has for you and you'll never go wrong.

I am truly one of the most fortunate of men to have a wife as wonderful as you, Janice. Thank you for keeping me on my knees, trusting God. Thank you for being so willing to embrace the adventure of life with me and to laugh our way down the path God has chosen for us. You bring such joy to my life. You are my best friend, and I love you now and always.

My deepest appreciation goes to my Savior and Lord, Jesus. Thank you, Lord, for choosing to use me and blessing me beyond what I deserve. I love you, Lord, and I am honored to be your servant.

Contents

Preface	…….……………………..	7
Chapter 1	The Gifts of the Spirit….........	9
Chapter 2	The Gift of Prophecy ….…......	20
Chapter 3	The Gift of Service ….…..……	34
Chapter 4	The Gift of Teaching….…..…..	48
Chapter 5	The Gift of Exhortation….…..	60
Chapter 6	The Gift of Giving …..…….….	73
Chapter 7	The Gift of Administration ...	86
Chapter 8	The Gift of Mercy….….….…..	100
Chapter 9	Living Your Gift….……..…...	115

Preface

What makes you different, distinct, from other people? Why do you relate to others the way you do? How can you maximize your joy and minimize your frustration?

I believe the reason so many people are frustrated is that they are focusing on what they can do, and not on who they are. Many of the conflicts within churches could be avoided if Christians understood what motivates each type of personality and the problems and abuses associated with each of the personality gifts.

Gifted For Life's Journey examines each of the seven personality gifts listed in Romans 12 and will help you discover the particular bent God has given you. Recognizing other's gifts will help you relate to your children, your spouse, and the people you deal with every day. Knowing your gift will give you an understanding of who you are and what God wants to accomplish in your life. It is my hope that you will use this workbook to help you discover your unique gift and exercise it for God's glory and His kingdom.

Sincerely His,

Chuck McAlister

Week One

The Gifts of the Spirit

Day One

Why are you the way that you are? What makes you different and distinct from every other person on earth? Why do you relate to others the way you do? How can you maximize your joy and minimize your frustration? Over the next few weeks, you will discover the answer to these questions and more.

Each of us has an inborn gift, given to us by God, which colors everything about us. The key to living in joy rather than frustration is discovering your special gift and then using it to serve God as He intended. Understanding the gifts of those around you – your spouse, your children, your friends, and fellow workers – will lead to more harmonious relationships as you begin to understand why others act and react in ways different than you.

The seven basic spiritual gifts are listed in Romans 12:6-8. "We have different gifts, according to the grace given us. If a man's gift is prophesying, let him use it in proportion to his faith. If it is serving, let him serve; if it is teaching, let him teach; if it is encouraging, let him encourage; if it is contributing to the needs of others, let him give generously; if it is leadership, let him govern diligently; if it is showing mercy, let him do it cheerfully." NIV

Each of these gifts correlates to a particular personality; therefore, these are called the *motivational gifts*. Every person has one of these seven gifts. In the following chapters we will examine each of the gifts in detail, looking in particular at three aspects: the personality of the gift, the problems of the gift, and the practice of the gift. We will see the good, the bad, and the ugly, as well as how each gift fits into the overall ministry of the local church.

God calls us to do three things in regard to these gifts: discover your gift, develop your gift, and display, or use, your gift. That's what this book is all about. This will be an interesting study, but it won't always be easy, so take your time and don't get frustrated. Begin by prayerfully asking the Holy Spirit to open your eyes and to allow you to see yourself as God sees you. Finally, allow Him to use you to His glory, just as He intended when He created you.

Definition of Spiritual Gifts

1 Peter 4:10 says, "Each one should use whatever gift he has received to serve others, faithfully administering God's grace in its various forms." NIV Peter's words *each one* include believers (those who have received Jesus Christ as their Lord and Savior) as well as non-believers (those who have not). Both believers and non-believers have a spirit, and both will live forever. The difference between them is that the Holy Spirit indwells the believers, and they will spend eternity in heaven with God when they die. The non-believers, because they do not have the Holy Spirit living within them, will spend eternity in hell. This place is described in the Bible as a lake of burning fire. Each of us must choose where we will spend eternity. Which would you rather have as your permanent address?

Why did God give us this gift, this spirit? Once we have been indwelt by the Holy Spirit, which energizes us, we are to minister our gift to one another. As we do so, we live out the manifold or multi-faceted grace of God. In this way we demonstrate that we have encountered the true, living God through His Son, Jesus Christ. This is the essence of salvation.

Genesis 1:26 tells us that man was made in the image of God. This means that not only did God create us, but He also gave us a spirit that reflects His own image. This God-given spirit makes us who we are; in other words, this is our personality.

Our spirit will live forever; it will never die, just as God will never die. This spirit was God's gift to mankind. Man is the only creature created in the image of God, and therefore the only one that has a spirit. It was an act of His grace and an example of His great love for us that caused Him to make us unique among all other creatures. So get ready to discover your own special gift in the weeks to come.

Day Two

Seven Facets of the Holy Spirit

In the book of Revelation, John describes his vision of heaven and the unveiling of Jesus Christ. He writes in Revelation 1:4, "John, to the seven churches which are in Asia: Grace be unto you and peace from Him who is and who was and who is to come, and from the seven Spirits which are before His throne."

The words *from Him* refer to God the Father, but who are the seven Spirits? Notice that the word *Spirits* is capitalized, indicating a proper noun, or a name. John is not saying that there are seven individual spirits around the throne of God, but rather he is giving us a vivid picture of the Holy Spirit.

John alludes to the Holy Spirit again in Revelation 3:1: "And to the angel of the church of Sardis write, 'These things say He who has the seven Spirits of God." We know that there is God the Father, God the Son, and God the Holy Spirit. This three-fold manifestation of God is known as the Trinity.

We also learn in this passage that the Holy Spirit exists in seven different facets. In other words, there are seven distinct expressions, or personalities, of the Holy Spirit. These personalities are the very same as the seven spiritual gifts listed in Romans 12.

There is a yearning within the heart of man to know God because He made us in His image. Our spirit is incomplete until the Spirit of God takes up residence within us; we need to be completed by God. There is a God-shaped void in every heart that only the Holy Spirit can fill. We cannot understand the truth of God until we are inhabited by the Holy Spirit of God.

Discover Your Gift

How can we discover our spiritual gift? There are three separate lists of gifts found in the New Testament. Romans 12, as we have seen, contains the motivational gifts. These define *who we are* as created in the image of God. Ephesians 4 contains the ministry gifts. These define *where we serve* as the result of the calling of God once we have come to know Him personally. 1 Corinthians 12 contains the manifestation gifts. These define *how we serve*. The power of the Holy Spirit is displayed through our service once we have come to know Jesus Christ personally.

Our personality expresses who we are, or our motivation. In Romans 12, we see the motivational gifts. These gifts influence you to do what you do–your motivational background. We will focus on this passage in this study because it helps us understand who we are.

Our place is where we serve, or our ministry. God gives us specific gifts of enabling. I know, for example, that I am called to be a pastor/teacher; however, I cannot fulfill that call of God unless I have a personal relationship with Jesus Christ. When I came to know Him personally, I was given a specific place of service by God. The gifts of service are listed for us in Ephesians 4.

Our power is how we serve, or the manifestation of our service. These gifts are listed for us in 1 Corinthians 12. They are the expression of God's Spirit operating in our lives after we have received the Holy Spirit through salvation. Once we are saved, we can express the power of Christ as the result of His moving through us.

In 1 Corinthians 12:4-7, Paul says "There are diversities of gifts...." That is our personality, or who we are. Then he says, "There are differences of ministries...." That is our place, or where we serve. Then in verse 6, Paul says, "And there are diversities of activities...." That is our power, or how we serve.

Paul includes all the different aspects of the gifts and how they function. The word for *gifts* is *charismata* in the Greek, which means grace. We are shaped by God's grace. The only reason we are who we are is that God had the grace to make us that way.

We sometimes don't like the way God made us. Remember, God is wiser than you or I, and He had a reason for making us as He did. He shaped and molded us in His image. There are seven diverse facets of the Holy Spirit, but He is the one and only Holy Spirit at work. He has a plan and a place for you, but it is up to you to find them.

The word for ministries in the Greek is *diakoniai.* It is the word from which we get our word *deacon,* and it means service. In other words, there are different ways and places of service, but there is the same Lord Jesus. He calls us, and we are to serve Him through His church.

Paul also describes a third area—diversities of activities. The word used for *activities* in the Greek is *energma* from which we get our word *energy*. This is the power that enables us to serve.

Paul says it is the same God in operation. First, there is the Holy Spirit with His seven distinct facets as expressed in the creation of man. Then there is the Lord Jesus Christ who calls His church to service and equips us to serve. And third, there is God the Father providing the power necessary to carry out the service. This is the Trinity—the Father, Son, and Holy Spirit—at work in our lives.

Notice that Paul writes in verse 7, "But the manifestation of the Spirit is given to each one for the profit of all." The word *manifestation* in the Greek is *phaneroosis.* It comes from a word that means lamp or lantern.

What does Paul mean? He is telling us that God lights our fire, then God helps us understand who we are. He then empowers us to serve where we need to serve. When that happens our fire is ignited as He works through us to accomplish His will, and we begin to burn as a flame for Almighty God!

It is important to see that we each have a personality that determines who we are because we were made in God's image. That is exactly what Paul was expressing when he said, "There are diversities of gifts, but the same Spirit."

We also have a place of service where God intends for us to serve. That is why Paul says, "There are differences of ministries," or service, "but there is the same Lord Jesus." Finally, we also have a power in the service God gives to us.

The Gifts of the Spirit

For this reason Paul says, "There are diversities of activities, but it is the same God that works all in all."

We cannot be the light we are called to be until we know who we are. Many Christians pray for God's power, but they do not really know who they are in Christ. They have not yet discovered how God created them—how He shaped them. These Christians find themselves extremely frustrated because they compare themselves to other Christians and feel inadequate. But they are not gifted to serve in the same ways many others are serving.

Perhaps God did not create them with the capacity to teach a Sunday school class or preach from the pulpit. God did not make us all the same, praise God! He gifted us in different ways so that every need within the body could be fulfilled.

No one is more valuable than anyone else. Every gift is equal and essential. Whatever personality type God has given us is created in His image. It is to be used to work out His will in our lives, and for the benefit of those whom we touch.

Many Christians are wasting their energy focusing on what they can do but not on who they are. I believe that, by the end of this workbook, you will have an understanding of just who you are and what God wants to do through you. You will have a vivid picture of what He wants to accomplish in your life.

You will also learn how to understand your boss, those you work with, and even that difficult person who bothers you so much. You will discover how to relate to others, because they too have a particular bent. Our gift is what gives us our personality. Our personality is beyond our control, because it was given to us at creation. It is the expression of the spirit God placed within us.

Even before a child comes to know Jesus Christ as his personal Lord and Savior, he already has a particular bent or personality. If parents can discover their child's personality type, (that part of the child that is an expression of the image of God) they will understand how to interact with and train that child.

I hope you are excited about this study. If you apply its truths, it can change your relationships for the better and improve your own life and work.

Day Three

How can we know God's will for our lives? How does God want to color our lives? What does He want the flavor of our lives to be? How does He want to shape us and mold us so that we become effective tools used by Him, with a capacity far greater than anything we ever imagined? To understand this, you must discover your spiritual gift. This is a five-step process.

First, make sure you are a Christian. Although those who are not saved are created in the image of God, they are not in touch with God, nor can they understand the truth of God. People never fully comprehend God's Word, the Bible, until they encounter their Creator through Jesus Christ. They do not know who they are, or that they are created as a unique individual. That is why they can be persuaded to believe that they evolved from a lower form. We are distinctive. God made us unique because He put the stamp of His Spirit upon us.

Second, confess all known sin. Sin grieves the Holy Spirit and quenches His power in our lives. It creates a barrier that hinders us from discovering our spiritual gift. It needs to be confessed and removed from our lives.

Third, present your bodies to God as a living sacrifice (Romans 12:1). We cannot find God's will unless we make a commitment to obey God in the minute details of our lives. This prepares us to recognize God's will. We compromise too often in areas that should not be negotiable. If we really want to be energized by the Spirit of God, we must be willing to obey God's will before we can discover His will.

Fourth, do not try to imitate someone else's gift. You cannot be someone else. God made you unique. I tried at one time to mimic other preachers. I would get their tapes, study their mannerisms, listen to the inflections in their voices, and do everything I could to copy them. But God made me just as I am, and I have to be willing to let God use me as I am. Trying to imitate others will only confuse you. Determine who *you* are.

Finally, study the characteristics of each gift. Those who share the same gift tend to have the same character traits. In the next chapters, we will go through each one of these gifts individually. One of these seven gifts will be yours.

The Seven Motivational Gifts

Now let's look at each of the seven gifts listed in Romans 12:6-8.

- *Prophecy*, in verse 6, is the ability to clearly perceive God's will. This is not the ability to foretell the future. A prophet proclaims God's Word to others.

- *Service* means helping, or ministering. The servant absolutely lives to serve others. It comes naturally to a server to ask, "How can I help? What can I do?"

The Gifts of the Spirit

- *Teaching* is the third gift. A teacher is one who loves to research and communicate truth. He is always searching for the truth.

- *Exhortation,* or encouragement, is the fourth gift. These are positive people who are always patting others on the back—in other words, the cheerleaders.

- *Giving* is the next gift. The giver looks for ways to give of his time, his resources, and himself in ways that are beyond the ordinary.

- *Administration* is gift number six. The administrator, or the leader, is the one who is gifted with the ability to organize even the most chaotic situation. This person also has a capacity for a broad vision. He can set long-range goals and take the steps necessary to reach those goals. He is good at assigning duties to others to accomplish a common purpose.

- The final gift is *mercy*, or the capacity for compassion and love. This person is drawn to those who are suffering or in need.

You now have a summary of the personality gifts. As we continue on through the study we will learn more about each gift and how to apply that knowledge to your daily life.

Day Four

Develop Your Gift

Someone wisely said, "What we are is God's gift to us. What we become is our gift to God." Once we discover our particular personality, we will be able to start developing who we are in Christ. We will be empowered by the Holy Spirit. The more we develop, the more power, influence, and fruit our lives will possess.

We will begin to understand things about ourselves that we never imagined. We will also understand why our spouses act the way they do. We will understand why our children respond as they do. They were all created with a particular bent. They were all shaped in a particular direction.

We will begin to serve the Lord with an overflow of joy because we will be filled with His Holy Spirit. He will work to a new depth in our lives that we

Gifted for Life's Journey

never thought possible. We will have tapped into the channel through which God's grace naturally flows in our lives.

When the Holy Spirit, with all seven facets of His expression, inhabits our lives, a connection is made between God and our spirit. That is the course through which God can flow naturally through us, just as water flows down the path of least resistance. We will find it easy to serve God because we will be energized by the Holy Spirit to allow Him to work through us. God made us so that His grace can pour out spiritually through the path of our particular gift.

In 1 Timothy 4:14 Paul advises Timothy, "Do not neglect the gift that is in you, which was given to you by prophecy with the laying on of the hands of the eldership." Paul reminds Timothy how he recognized his gift. The word *given* in the Greek is the word *didomi,* which means to discover.

Someone with the gift of prophesy probably came to Timothy and said, "I can see by the way you are living your life that you have this particular gift." That insight energized Timothy, who then set about serving God with his gift.

Paul also told Timothy that he was ordained, or set apart, for his place of service and should develop or grow in that gift. In 2 Timothy 1:6 Paul says, "Therefore I remind you to stir up the gift of God which is in you through the laying on of my hands." Paul had laid his hands on Timothy and ordained him for the purpose of service.

The words *stir up* are in the present tense and mean to rekindle or refire. The Holy Spirit rekindles, or energizes, our spirit and gives us a unique spiritual gift with which we are to serve Him. This is an expression of His power working through our lives and is only available to those who are saved.

God makes each one of us unique, and everyone will view situations differently. For example, let's say that there are seven people sitting around a dinner table, each one with a different gift. As the hostess is carrying the dessert into the dining room, she trips. The tray falls and shatters, leaving a mess on the floor. How will each of the seven people react?

- The prophet will say, "That's what happens when you're not careful." His motivation is to correct the problem that caused the situation.

- The servant will say, "Let me help you clean that up." Her motivation is to meet an immediate need.

- The *teacher* will expound on the reason the hostess tripped and the dessert landed upside down instead of right side up. His motivation is to explain why it happened.

- The exhorter will say, "Don't worry about it. Everything will be fine. The next time, we'll eat in the kitchen and you won't need to carry the tray in

16

The Gifts of the Spirit

here." His motivation is to encourage the hostess and offer advice for the future.

- The giver will say, "I'll go out right now and buy another dessert." His motivation is to find a way to meet the need.

- The administrator will immediately say, "Jim, get the mop. Sue, you help clean this up. Sam, bring another tray of desert from the kitchen." He will quickly take control of the situation. His motivation is to provide leadership to meet the needs of the group.

- The mercy-giver will take the hand of the hostess and say, "I know you feel bad, but it could happen to anyone. Please don't let it bother you." His motivation would be to relieve her embarrassment.

Each reaction is very different. We can be tempted to look at someone else and think, "What's wrong with him? Why doesn't he respond to situations the same way I do?" The inherent danger is that you will condemn those who react differently than you. Always remember that God did not make everyone like you, and God did not make you to be like everyone else. God made you distinctly different so that He could use you effectively for Jesus Christ in whatever situation you find yourself.

How do you develop your gift? First, determine the particular gift God gave you when He created you, and then begin to study and grow in that area. That is exactly what this study will help you do.

You must also identify the gifts in which you are weaker so that you can grow in those areas. I know, for example, that my weakest area is mercy, and unless I am maturing in that area, I am not growing spiritually. The Holy Spirit exhibits all seven personalities, and until we do the same, we will not know Him in His fullness.

The by-product of being able to develop ourselves according to our bent is an overwhelming sense of joy because we are being used by Almighty God. We are to identify our own gift and exercise that gift so that we become a channel through which God's grace can flow. That is what it means to develop your gift.

Next, we will see how to recognize each gift in action. This is when you will begin to spot and appreciate the different gifts in your family and acquaintances.

17

Gifted for Life's Journey

| Day Five |

Display Your Gift

Not only are we called to discover, and develop our gift, but we are also called to display our gift. We are meant to use our gifts to help each other and work together for the good of God's kingdom.

The Scriptures have a teaching for every one of the seven gifts. They admonish us as Christians to develop ourselves in each area. We may not have the gift of prophesy, but Hebrews 5:14 instructs us to discern the truth. We are told in Galatians 5:13 to serve one another. We are to teach one another, according to Colossians 3:16, even though we may not be gifted as a teacher.

There are many things we can learn from each other. The areas in which you are gifted will come easier for you, while other areas will prove more difficult. That is where you start the process of maturing.

Let me give you a brief idea of how each personality views the church. These different personalities can create friction within the church from time to time, because each feels that the church's ministries should operate a particular way.

- The prophet, for example, when expressing what he thinks ought to be the main emphasis of the church, might say, "We need a pastor who preaches the Word of God and is not afraid to expose sin."

- The server might say, "We need to have a good benevolence ministry. Helping others is the key to meeting the needs of the body."

- The teacher may say, "We need more in-depth Bible study. The church must be grounded in the truth."

- The exhorter will say, "We need a strong personal counseling and discipleship ministry that encourages believers to become spiritually mature."

- The giver says, "We need to emphasize stewardship so we can have a generous program of giving to support our ministries and missions."

- The administrator might say, "We need effective processes, an accurate budget, and an efficient organization."

- The one who has the gift of mercy will say, "We need to be a caring church. We should reach out to people who are hurting."

All seven of these viewpoints are correct and express characteristics that a New Testament church should have, and all seven are vital and necessary. If we are not careful, we will focus only on areas we think are important, and we will not allow the ministry of the church to be accomplished in all of the areas God wants to work.

The ultimate purpose of displaying our gifts is to benefit others. It is not just so that we can find out who we are, nor is it only so that we can discover how we will feel more fulfilled. It is so that we can understand how God wants to use us in the greatest capacity for His kingdom. If we are only using our gifts to fulfill our own desires and wants, then we are abusing our gifts.

You cannot be a spectator and learn what God wants to teach you through this study. You must be willing to become involved. For some reason, the church, particularly in America, has moved to the point of allowing its members to be passive spectators. It amazes me that our churches may be full on Sunday mornings, but many live the rest of the week like those who aren't Christians.

So many people think, "I've done my part, I've punched my ticket, and I've given God His due. Therefore, I can go on about my life assured that God will take care of me." The church building is not the only place where service is done. We are to serve God wherever we are.

The energizing of the Holy Spirit occurs so that you can live your life having been confronted, corrected, encouraged, and empowered by the Word of God. Then you are thrust into the real world so that you can make a difference for Jesus Christ. That is what God has called us to do.

This study is not for those who want to sit back and be complacent. It is for those who say, "Lord, I really want you to use me beyond any capacity you have ever used me before."

I encourage you to make a commitment to study, to learn, and to apply the truth as God empowers you to discover not only who you are, but what He can do through you. Are you ready and willing to do that?

Week Two

The Gift of Prophecy

...if prophecy, let us prophesy in proportion to our faith; Romans 12:6

Day One

Let's begin this week by studying the first of seven motivational gifts listed in Romans 12:6—the gift of prophesy. Each week we will look at the personality of a particular gift, as well as its practice, and the problems associated with the gift. This is the way the gift is used and the way the gift is abused.

As you study the personality traits of each gift, circle the number under each statement that best describes you. If a statement is always true in your life, circle 5. If it is never true, circle 0. If it is somewhere in between, circle the appropriate number. At the end of each week there is a page to copy and total your scores for each gift. After completing this study, you will know which gift belongs to you.

The word *prophecy* in Romans 12:6 refers to a person who perceives God's will and proclaims it to others. Please don't get the wrong idea. This does not mean the ability to foretell or predict the future. Following are ten personality traits of the gift of prophecy.

The Personality of the Prophet

First, someone with the gift of prophesy sees everything as black or white, either in or out of God's will. There are no gray areas. A prophet can quickly evaluate a situation and accurately identify good and evil.

It is difficult for a prophet to accept compromise between right and wrong. He tends to be extreme in his feelings and in his words and can exhibit an intense hatred for evil. In fact, the prophet has a desire to overcome and eliminate evil in whatever form it appears.

The Gift of Prophecy

►**A prophet sees everything as black or white, either in or out of God's will.**

Rate yourself:

	Never	Seldom	Sometimes	Usually	Mostly	Always
	0	1	2	3	4	5

A prophet feels a need to express his ideas regarding right and wrong and will often do so on the spur of the moment. You can count on a prophet to tell you what he thinks. He normally forms a quick opinion and is able to offer an assessment of any situation because he operates from a strong inner conviction about good and evil.

A prophet can be very persuasive, even overpowering at times. He also tends to have a lot to say, and is usually right when he is operating on the basis of the Holy Spirit. A prophet normally does not mince words. He speaks directly to a situation and is very frank. Because he is so outspoken, the prophet is not a boring person, and there is often a certain dramatic flair about him.

He is driven to see immediate results. When he confronts evil, he wants it attacked and conquered. When he promotes good, he wants to see that good advanced and victorious.

When a prophet sees a problem, he wants it solved. Someone with the gift of mercy says, "Let's work through it," but a prophet says, "Let's get this thing fixed." He is driven by the desire to see the problem corrected.

The prophet is so perceptive that he can make decisions and answer questions quickly with a yes or no, and he will seldom give indefinite answers. He is very good at making snap judgments and quick evaluations. He can usually walk into a room and discern what is going on, not by outward analysis, but by virtue of his prophetic gift.

As we study the gifts, we will look at Biblical figures who display the specific characteristics of each gift. It is no surprise that the person who especially displays the characteristics of a prophet is Simon Peter. He was able to quickly size up any situation and decide what needed to be done.

When he saw Jesus walking across the water, he called out to Jesus, then without hesitation, stepped in, and went to meet Him. It was Simon Peter who spoke for all the disciples at Pentecost and directly addressed the wrong his audience had committed. In Acts 2:23, he identifies the very ones who crucified Jesus and said, "Him, you have taken by lawless hands, have crucified, and put to death." Simon Peter accurately and quickly assessed the group to whom he was speaking and fearlessly proclaimed the truth.

Gifted for Life's Journey

Later on, as he was examined by a ruling council, he immediately expressed his ideas about right and wrong. Acts 4:10 reads, "...let it be known to you all, and to all the people of Israel, that by the name of Jesus Christ of Nazareth, Whom you crucified, Whom God raised form the dead, by Him this man stands here before you whole." The rulers could not intimidate Peter. He stood up for what was right because he had a burning desire to express his inner conviction at that very place and time.

▶ **A prophet feels a need to express his ideas regarding right and wrong and will often do so on the spur of the moment.**

Rate yourself:	Never	Seldom	Sometimes	Usually	Mostly	Always
	0	1	2	3	4	5

Day Two

A prophet is uniquely gifted to spot hypocrisy in others and will be extremely direct when confronting it. Because of his keen perception, a prophet is always looking beyond a given situation. Don't be hypocritical around a prophet. When a prophet hears someone saying one thing and knows that he is acting another way, the prophet is absolutely driven to confront that person. It doesn't matter who or what it is, a prophet has to do something about it.

For example, if someone claims to be a church leader but does not attend church regularly, that's a form of hypocrisy. The prophet feels he must confront it. That is the way God made him. A prophet is compelled to expose sin wherever he sees it.

A prophet acts out of compassion and not out of a desire to hurt someone. He knows that sin always results in consequences, even though it may only become apparent much later. He operates with a spiritual scalpel. He exposes a situation, examines it, diagnoses the problem, and prescribes a remedy to correct the situation in order to prevent further harm.

Many people don't understand the simplistic solutions a prophet offers to complex problems because they don't understand how a prophet's mind works. A prophet is motivated to see that the right thing is done. He will grieve over another's sin because he knows the consequences sin carries.

He does not care what others think of him and is willing to risk the anger of others to insure that sin is dealt with. A person with the gift of service or the gift of mercy is people-oriented and doesn't want anyone to be upset with him,

The Gift of Prophecy

but the prophet will confront sin so that God's will can be done, even if it means losing a friend.

In the account of Ananias and Sapphira in Acts 5:3-4, Peter says, "...Ananias, why has Satan filled your heart to lie to the Holy Spirit and keep back part of the price of the land for yourself?... You have not lied to men but to God."

When it came to spotting hypocrisy in others, Simon Peter was extremely direct. When he dealt with Ananias and Sapphira, Peter didn't form a committee to decide if Ananias really gave all of the money as he claimed. No, he went directly to Ananias. Peter was saying, "I can't believe your hypocrisy. You are lying to God. How can you do this?" That is the way a prophet thinks. He is motivated to confront any type of hypocrisy.

▶ **A prophet is uniquely gifted to spot hypocrisy in others and will be extremely direct when confronting it.**

Rate yourself:	Never	Seldom	Sometimes	Usually	Mostly	Always
	0	1	2	3	4	5

A prophet has very strong convictions and strict personal standards. He can usually be counted on, unless he is in the flesh, to display impeccable morals and absolute honesty. He has an opinion on almost everything, and he can be totally, even brutally, frank. He values integrity and is aware of the presence of the Lord. More than anything else, the motivation for his life is to please God.

Once again, Peter exemplifies the prophet. He was brought before the Jewish council several times for preaching the gospel. In Acts 5:28-29 the high priest says, "Did we not strictly command you not to teach in this name? And look, you have filled Jerusalem with your doctrine, and intend to bring this Man's blood on us!" But Peter and the other apostles answered and said: "We ought to obey God rather than men."

Peter's response in verse 29 was spoken like a true prophet. "I'm not trying to please you. I'm going to do God's will whether you like it or not."

▶ **A prophet has strong convictions and strict personal standards.**

Rate yourself:	Never	Seldom	Sometimes	Usually	Mostly	Always
	0	1	2	3	4	5

Gifted for Life's Journey

Day Three

A prophet is open in expressing his own faults and accepting brokenness as God's way of working in his life. He would rather be humiliated than to be in sin. A prophet understands that God breaks our stubborn will to make us usable.

Don't look for sympathy from a prophet. He will probably say, "Praise God, what an opportunity for growth! What is God teaching you?" That is not what a person in the midst of suffering wants to hear.

Being a prophet myself, I have to suppress the urge to respond this way. Having encountered tragedy, however I have learned that God teaches us deep truths through sorrow. When someone describes a difficult experience, I become excited, because I know God is going to do a great work in his life.

Those of you with the gift of mercy probably don't understand this. Your primary motivation is sharing others' hurts to relieve their pain. But if you are a prophet, your primary motivation is to help others see the spiritual lesson to be learned.

A prophet views difficult experiences as proof that God loves us enough to teach us and shape us into the people He knows we can be. It is almost as if a prophet must be hurt before he adequately understands what God wants to teach him. I know that is not pleasant, but it is part of the process of growth in the life of a prophet. He must be willing to experience brokenness so that he can grow spiritually. A prophet ultimately learns how to rejoice in brokenness.

In order to grow, he must be willing to express the brokenness he is going through. He is usually willing to be an open book, which allows him to be transparent. You don't have to worry about a prophet trying to promote a hidden agenda or do any secret maneuvering behind the scenes. The prophet doesn't like to manipulate others. All he understands is that God's direction is the only option there is for him.

On one occasion Peter was so overcome with his own sin that he fell at Jesus' feet and said in Luke 5:8, "Depart from me, for I am a sinful man, O Lord!" When a prophet finds evil, he is compelled to deal with it. When he finds evil in his own life, he would rather be broken by God than have sin remain in his life.

In John 13:8-9 Peter says, "You shall never wash my feet!" Jesus answered him, "If I do not wash you, you have no part with Me." Simon Peter said to Him, "Lord, not my feet only, but also my hands and my head!" That's a typical prophet's response. If that is what God wants to do, then let's go all the way. Peter accepted God's will whole-heartedly.

The Gift of Prophecy

►A prophet is open in expressing his own faults and accepting brokenness as God's way of working in his life.

Rate yourself:	Never	Seldom	Sometimes	Usually	Mostly	Always
	0	1	2	3	4	5

A prophet has a genuine concern to see God's will done and will defend God's will, even when it means personal suffering. A prophet wants to do God's will above all else and desires to be obedient to God at all costs. A prophet living in the Spirit is willing to go to great lengths to be in the will of God.

Acts 5:40-42 records that the counsel beat Peter and the other apostles and " ... they commanded that they should not speak in the name of Jesus, and let them go. So they departed from the presence of the council rejoicing that they were counted worthy to suffer shame for His name. And daily in the temple, and in every house, they did not cease teaching and preaching Jesus as the Christ." Why? Because Peter was driven to see God's will accomplished.

►A prophet has a genuine concern to see God's will done and will defend God's will, even when it means personal suffering.

Rate yourself:	Never	Seldom	Sometimes	Usually	Mostly	Always
	0	1	2	3	4	5

A prophet views God's Word as the source of his convictions and the basis for all truth, action, and authority. He loves God's Word; loves to study it, pray over it, and hear God speaking to him through it. When Peter preaches, we see a message saturated with the understanding of scripture. He quoted the Old Testament again and again.

A prophet does not want to hear what other people think. He wants to hear what the Word of God says. When a prophet is sensitive to God's Word, he follows God's will and not the majority consensus.

He usually has a good command of words and knows how to make a point. A prophet in the Spirit can be very authoritative, and his family will respect what he has to say.

Gifted for Life's Journey

► **A prophet views God's Word as the source of his convictions and the basis for all truth, action, and authority.**

Rate yourself:	Never	Seldom	Sometimes	Usually	Mostly	Always
	0	1	2	3	4	5

Day Four

A prophet has few or no personal friends. The life of a prophet is usually marked by loneliness. He may go through childhood with only one or two close friends. Broad friendships require a great deal of tolerance, and a prophet has a hard time tolerating those who have weak convictions.

A prophet can be very introspective. You will rarely know, but he is usually struggling with self-image problems and can be very hard on himself. Many times he feels as if he does not fit in with his surroundings.

Whenever I teach about spiritual gifts, the prophets in the class are more excited about discovering their gift than anyone else. They are thrilled when they realize that God really does have a place for them and that they are not misfits.

God has provided the prophet with something that helps conquer his image problem: prayer. A prophet has to pray constantly to maintain a strong awareness of God's presence in his life. There is something in the heart of a prophet that drives him to pray consistently. He is compelled to discern God's will, not so that he can change it, but simply so that he can engage the Lord in prayer.

Nowhere in Scripture do we read that Peter had close friends. He was alone when Andrew came to take him to meet Jesus. A prophet enjoys spending time alone with God and allowing Him to cleanse his heart. Because a prophet is so concerned with establishing God's will for his life and spending time in prayer, he does not take time for numerous personal relationships.

► **A prophet has few or no personal friends.**

Rate yourself:	Never	Seldom	Sometimes	Usually	Mostly	Always
	0	1	2	3	4	5

The Gift of Prophecy

A prophet exhibits loyalty and commitment without reservations. He may confront you about the sin he has seen in your life, but he will not desert you. Many times a prophet will remain devoted to the point of getting himself into trouble. He wants to have an impact on a person's life and help him be free from the sin encroaching upon him.

Peter expressed great loyalty at the Last Supper when Jesus informed the disciples that one of them would betray Him. Jesus told Peter, "Before the rooster crows, you will deny Me three times." Simon Peter leaned over and said to Jesus, "Even if I have to die with You, I will not deny You!" Peter could not imagine denying Jesus because he was so intensely devoted to Him.

At the time Roman soldiers came to arrest Jesus in the garden of Gethsemane, Peter drew his sword and promptly cut off a soldier's ear. He was prepared to take on the whole Roman army on behalf of Jesus. That is the way a prophet is bent. Later, when he failed and showed disloyalty to Jesus by denying Him, Peter was wounded to his very heart and was nearly overwhelmed by remorse.

► **A prophet exhibits loyalty and commitment without reservations.**

Rate yourself:	Never	Seldom	Sometimes	Usually	Mostly	Always
	0	1	2	3	4	5

A prophet operates with boldness, and his words and actions can be daring. He is a person of strong principle. While continuing to uphold the righteousness of God, he should learn to temper his boldness with graciousness so as not to seem abrasive.

Jesus asked His disciples in Matthew 16:16, "Who do men say that I am?" Peter immediately said, "You are the Christ, the son of the living God." He spoke and acted as a prophet. A prophet isn't afraid to take a stand.

► **A prophet operates with boldness.**

Rate yourself:	Never	Seldom	Sometimes	Usually	Mostly	Always
	0	1	2	3	4	5

Gifted for Life's Journey

Your Score on the Gift of Prophecy

Take a few moments now to look back and copy your scores for this week on the characteristics of the gift of prophecy. Add up your total points for the gift and record it at the bottom of the page. You will do this for each one of the gifts, and by the time you complete this study, you will be able to identify your own gift.

_4_ A prophet sees everything as black or white, either in or out of God's will.

_2_ A prophet feels a need to express his ideas regarding right and wrong and will often do so on the spur of the moment.

_2_ A prophet is uniquely gifted to spot hypocrisy in others and will be extremely direct when confronting it.

_4_ A prophet has strong convictions and strict personal standards.

_4_ A prophet is open in expressing his own faults and accepting brokenness as God's way of working in his life.

_2_ A prophet has a genuine concern to see God's will done and will defend God's will, even when it means personal suffering.

_5_ A prophet views the Bible as the source of his convictions and the basis of all truth, action, and authority.

_4_ A prophet has few or no close friends.

_5_ A prophet exhibits loyalty and commitment without reservations.

_4_ A prophet operates with boldness.

~~3~~ ~~3~~ 6 Total Points

The Gift of Prophecy

Day Five

Today we will take an overall look at the gift of prophecy. We'll see what can go wrong with this gift and also what can go right with the gift of prophecy. We will also look at ways to deal with a child with this gift. Parents, teachers, and family members will find this immensely helpful.

The Problems of the Gift of Prophecy

Because a prophet has a way with words, he knows just what to say to cut and to hurt others deeply. If you have determined that you are bent in this direction, you must be especially careful because a prophet living in the flesh can devastate his family. He can be so severe, so harsh, and so compulsive in his correction that he can damage the ones he loves.

A prophet is often misunderstood because of his frankness. His forthright comments may be misinterpreted as harshness. An immature prophet can be abrupt and may not be able to express himself without seeming somewhat intolerant or severe.

Many times people around a prophet will take his confrontation of sin as being uncaring. They do not understand how deeply a prophet does care and how profoundly he is wounded by the sin he sees in other people's lives.

The Practice of the Gift of Prophecy

A Prophet in the Spirit

There are seven ways to tell if a prophet is operating in accordance with God's will. When you recognize one of these characteristics, you know that person is living by the power of the Holy Spirit.

Gifted for Life's Journey

Boldness

Drawing his authority from the Word of God, he will be bold in his stance and remain obedient to God. There will be no blinking in the face of sin, and he will not be intimidated. It does not matter to him what other people think.

Purity

When operating in the Spirit, he would rather die than tolerate sin in his life. Purity will be evident in his speech, in what he reads, and in where he goes. His testimony will be intact.

Do not tell a dirty joke to a prophet or say a curse word in his presence. You will hurt him more than you could ever imagine. A prophet operating in the power of the Spirit is striving to demonstrate purity in his own life.

Commitment

He is committed to God's Word and the important things in his life. You will never see a prophet who is operating in the Spirit desert his spouse, his family, or his church.

Sincerity

A prophet doesn't play games. He is compelled to be transparent and real. There is nothing phony or hypocritical about him when he is in the Spirit.

Persuasiveness

A prophet in the Spirit can be very appealing. He can be very influential, especially to another person who is sensitive to the Holy Spirit.

Forgiveness

Even though a prophet is quick to confront sin, he is also quick to forgive if repentance is evident. Regardless of what you have done to a prophet, if you demonstrate a repentant heart, that prophet will be willing to forgive you when he is operating in the Spirit.

Joy

The joy of the Lord is evident in his life.

The Gift of Prophecy

A Prophet in the Flesh

There are also seven ways to tell when a prophet is operating in the flesh. When you see one of these seven characteristics, you know that a prophet has stepped over the line. He has begun to operate on the basis of his own flesh, not on the basis of the Spirit.

Fear

You can see his anxiety. He operates with fear and dread. He worries about what people think instead of being guided by the Holy Spirit.

Wickedness

A prophet operating in the flesh becomes extremely sensual. I am convinced that many of the preachers who have fallen into immoral activities have been prophets operating in the flesh. A prophet has to be constantly on guard of his own heart, his own life, and his own family, to insure that he does not drift into sensuality.

Indecisiveness

A prophet operating in the flesh cannot make a decision. He will lose confidence in his own judgment and hesitate to make a commitment or take a stand.

Hypocrisy

He refuses to be transparent and tries to hide his actions. He becomes deceptive and camouflages his motives. He is no longer an open book and does not allow you to see into his heart. Many times it is because his heart has been broken and he did not assimilate that brokenness in a spiritual way, but instead chose to operate on the basis of the flesh. He professes one thing but does another.

Demanding

A prophet operating in the flesh will be determined to have his own way. He may say things like, "I am the man of this house. I pay the bills in this place. You do what I say, when I say to do it." He begins to operate on the basis of dictatorial control rather than the authority granted to him by God.

Bitterness

Sometimes a prophet will refuse to forgive. One who is operating in the flesh can devastate his loved ones. He will feel rejected and think others are talking about him. A prophet is somewhat of a loner anyway, but rather than being content in that solitary state and moving closer to God, he will carry a chip on his shoulder.

Frustration

A prophet operating in the flesh will be overcome by anger. He will feel frustrated, irritable, and weary, and he will have no joy.

Peter's Example

Peter was a good illustration of a prophet operating in the Spirit one minute and in the flesh the next. His most disappointing moment was when he denied Jesus Christ and swore three times he didn't even know Him.

Jesus later appeared to Simon Peter on the shore of the Sea of Galilee and asked him three times, "Simon Peter, do you love Me?" In the Greek, we find that Jesus used the word *agape* the first time. This word denotes the love of God.

Simon Peter said, "Lord, you know that I love you." But he used a different word, the word *phileo,* which means brotherly love. Simon Peter could not bring himself to admit the deep love that he had for God. In his humiliation he said, "Lord, all I can do is offer to You my brotherly love because I have already failed once. Surely I'll fail again."

Jesus asked Simon Peter a second time, "Do you *agape* Me?" And Peter looked back at Jesus and said that second time, "Oh Lord, I *phileo* You. I love You as a brother, but I know I will fail You again. I am not even worthy to be in Your presence." Then with the love and compassion that only Jesus can have, He looked at Simon Peter the third time and said, "Simon Peter, do you *phileo* Me? Do you love Me like that?" You can almost sense the relief in Simon Peter when he says, "Oh yes, Lord I do, I love You."

Dealing With a Prophet as a Child

Proverbs 22:6 says, "Train up a child in the way he should go." In the Hebrew this means to train up a child according to his bent; to discover his bent and learn how to deal with him accordingly. Let's look at the gift of prophecy in the context of this verse.

If you have a strong-willed child, one who is obstinately set on having his own way, then you probably have a prophet on your hands. If that is the case, the child must be strongly disciplined and brought to the point of submission. If not,

The Gift of Prophecy

he will grow up to be an arrogant adult who says, "I am going to have my own way whenever I want it."

It is imperative that you begin immediately to correct him, to shape him, and to mold him with an accurate understanding of who he is. Unless you teach him submission, his gift will be polluted, and you are going to have a tremendous problem. He will become a prophet living in the flesh instead of living in the power of the Spirit of God.

But don't give up hope for your strong-willed child, for if God can reach the heart of a prophet like Peter, He can surely reach your child's heart too.

Week Three

The Gift of Service

...or ministry, let us use it in our ministering... Romans 12:7

Day One

This week we will look at the second spiritual gift listed in Romans 12, the gift of service. At first glance this gift may seem self-explanatory; however, we will see that there's more to this gift than meets the eye.

The gift of service, or ministry, is listed after prophecy in Romans 12:7. The word for ministry in the Greek is *diakonia,* and it carries with it the idea of doing practical things to meet the needs of others. A person who is bent in this direction is alert and sensitive to the practical needs of others. He seems to have built-in radar that immediately detects needs. We will begin by looking at ten personality traits of a server.

The Personality of the Server

A server quickly spots a practical need and feels compelled to meet that need in a swift and meticulous manner. A server is easy to recognize around the church. He is the one who is scurrying about, setting up tables, moving chairs, and doing other practical things to meet needs. At home, she is usually busy in the kitchen or doing something in the workshop. You can make a casual comment to a server about a need, and he will feel compelled to try to meet it.

A person who is bent in this direction has a strong belief that actions speak louder than words. He may not tell you how much he loves you, but he will *show* you how much he loves you by what he does for you. That is the best way he knows to express love.

Timothy is a biblical example of the server. In Philippians 2:19-20, Paul writes, "But I trust in the Lord Jesus to send Timothy to you shortly, that I also may be encouraged when I know your state. For I have no one like-minded, who

The Gift of Service

will sincerely care for your state." In other words, Paul says, "I don't have anyone else like him whose natural gift is to look for ways to care for you." Paul knew that Timothy's gift was service.

▶ **A server quickly spots a practical need and feels compelled to meet that need in a swift and meticulous manner .**

Rate yourself:	Never	Seldom	Sometimes	Usually	Mostly	Always
	0	1	2	3	4	5

A server derives joy and a sense of purpose in serving others beyond the expected. Serving is the essence of Christianity to a server, and everything else is empty words. A server may judge other Christians based on whether or not they are involved in meeting the practical needs of other people. He can't understand why everyone else isn't quick to roll up their sleeves and dive in to take care of needs.

We all tend to view life through our own colored glasses. As a prophet, I find myself wondering, "How can he be so compassionate? Doesn't he know that person is living in sin and needs to get his life right with God?" If you are a prophet, you are probably thinking, "Amen!" We must be careful not to assume that everyone sees a situation exactly as we do.

A server enjoys doing more than expected. When there is a need he will meet the need, and then he will find a way to go the extra mile. There is something inside a server that motivates him to go above and beyond the expected to help others. His joy comes from doing something helpful.

Timothy was that kind of person. In Philippians 2:21-22, Paul said, "For all seek their own, not the things which are of Christ Jesus. But you know his proven character, that as a son with his father he served with me in the gospel."

Paul meant, "Timothy has been like my son. He served with me, allowing me to be more effective in communicating the gospel." A server loves to do the practical things that help others.

▶ **A server derives joy and a sense of purpose in serving others beyond the expected.**

Rate yourself:	Never	Seldom	Sometimes	Usually	Mostly	Always
	0	1	2	3	4	5

Gifted for Life's Journey

Day Two

A server tends to sacrifice his own needs, even personal health, to serve others. There is an old adage that it's always the plumber's pipes that leak and the painter's house that needs painting. That describes a server, because he has only one thing on his mind— meeting the needs of others. A server doesn't think about himself or his own needs. He can be absolutely untiring, and it is amazing what he can do and how far he can go.

Many times he will neglect his own family in order to meet someone else's need. His spouse may have to say, "Stop and take a look at what you are doing. You're taking care of everyone else, but you're overlooking our own family!"

A server will postpone going to the doctor or finding time to rest because he is just too busy. He is always thinking of something else that he could do to meet another's need.

In 1 Timothy 5:23, Paul advises Timothy, "No longer drink only water, but use a little wine for your stomach's sake and your frequent infirmities." Timothy's physical problems were probably related to his gift. He was often expending much of his energy to meet the needs of others, and he wasn't taking care of himself.

▶ **A server tends to sacrifice his own needs, even personal health, to serve others.**

Rate yourself:	Never	Seldom	Sometimes	Usually	Mostly	Always
	0	1	2	3	4	5

A server has difficulty saying *no* to requests for help. The server is so geared to serve that he tends to become overloaded very quickly. If you ask him how to unclog a drain, he will soon be under your sink with a wrench in his hand taking care of your problem. He usually ends up on a dozen different committees, side-tracked into all sorts of tasks. Many times he forgets to pray about where God wants him to be involved, and he volunteers for every job that comes along.

One reason a server can become frustrated is because he is an absolute perfectionist. He wants everything he is involved in done perfectly. He will work hard to make sure that every *i* is dotted and every *t* is crossed.

If this is your gift, make sure that you maintain an intimate fellowship with the Lord so you can determine the precise projects He wants you to take on.

The Gift of Service

If you don't, you will easily find yourself becoming frustrated and burned out. God can teach you how to say "no". It is important for you as a server to learn to prioritize your life.

Paul had to continually admonish Timothy not to overwork himself and to keep his focus. Two letters in the New Testament were specifically written to Timothy about how to keep from being side-tracked as he served the Lord.

In 2 Timothy 2:3-4, Paul told Timothy, "You therefore must endure hardship as a good soldier of Jesus Christ. No one engaged in warfare entangles himself with the affairs of this life, that he may please him who enlisted him as a soldier." Paul's advice was to be careful and don't get so wrapped up in serving that you forget that your primary calling is to maintain fellowship with God.

▶ **A server has difficulty saying "no" to requests for help.**

Rate yourself:	Never	Seldom	Sometimes	Usually	Mostly	Always
	0	1	2	3	4	5

A server enjoys manual projects that combine attention to detail with a good memory. The server has a remarkable ability to work well with his hands, and he is always doing projects. Usually a husband who is a server has a workshop and loves to make or fix things. He likes to go on mission trips that involve construction projects. He can do just about anything that requires manual labor or working with his hands. A server seldom likes to sit at a desk unless he feels useful.

A server loves to give meticulous attention to detail. He can't stand clutter or disorganization. A woman, for example, who is bent in this direction may dust her house continuously. Every bed will be made up as soon as the family is awake. If you drop in to visit, there will be no dirty dishes in the sink, and her home is usually neat.

Ladies, you may not believe this, but there really are men who don't throw their clothes around; they put them in the hamper instead. They have the gift of service. Have you ever seen a guy who draws little patterns on the wall of his workshop for his tools? You know when a tool is missing because the outline is there but the tool is gone. That man probably has the gift of service.

A server says things like, "I just can't leave my office until my desk is cleared." Or he may say, "I have a hard time going to Joe's house," and you know he is thinking, "I could have that place straightened up in fifteen minutes if he would let me." A server will walk around your house and straighten up the picture frames on the wall. He cannot stand for things to be out of order. That is part of his calling because that is the way he is bent.

Gifted for Life's Journey

Many servers are blessed with a great memory for detail. A secretary with the gift of service will remember how her boss likes his coffee. If your friend is a server, she will remember your favorite dessert. That is because it helps her enhance her service to you. She derives pleasure from finding ways to meet your needs because that is the way God made her. That is something we all can learn from servers.

When Paul had specific needs, he knew he could ask Timothy for help because Timothy would remember the details. Paul says in 2 Timothy 4:13 "Bring the cloak that I left with Carpus at Troas when you come, and the books, especially the parchments." Paul knew he could ask Timothy to bring those things, and that he would take care of it because service was Timothy's gift.

▶ **A server enjoys manual projects that combine attention to detail with a remarkable memory.**

Rate yourself:	Never	Seldom	Sometimes	Usually	Mostly	Always
	0	1	2	3	4	5

Day Three

A server needs communication of specific instructions before service is rendered and wants to be shown appreciation afterwards. A server becomes extremely frustrated if you don't tell him what you expect of him. This is an area that is very sensitive to a person who has the gift of service. He needs to know from the start what is required to accomplish a task. Once the task is completed, he also needs to know how much you appreciate him and his meticulous attention to detail. He wants to be confident that his efforts will not be wasted and that you will appreciate what he is doing.

A server can be misunderstood at this point because people may assume that he is only serving in order to be praised; that is not the case. He needs to be praised because your appreciation confirms the validity of his service, and he wants to know that he is meeting your needs. A server does not want to waste his effort or his energy. He likes to know that what he is doing is important to you and that it actually does take care of your need.

Paul gave Timothy more instruction and more praise than any other person in Scripture. Two books in the New Testament are dedicated to Timothy. Paul even told others to make sure that they expressed appreciation to him. In 1 Corinthians 16:10-11 Paul writes, "And if Timothy comes, see that he may be with you without fear." You can see how much Paul loved Timothy. He is telling

The Gift of Service

the believers at Corinth to take care of him and not to let him be fearful. Paul reminds them, "...for he does the work of the Lord, as I also do."

Paul describes Timothy as a server. "Therefore let no one despise him. But send him on his journey in peace, that he may come to me; for I am waiting for him with the brethren (1 Corinthians 16:11)." Paul asks them to express appreciation for the work Timothy does. One with the personality of a server is stirred by expressions of appreciation. If he knows you are pleased, he will desire to work even harder.

▶ **A server needs communication of specific instructions before service is rendered and appreciation afterwards.**

Rate yourself:	Never	Seldom	Sometimes	Usually	Mostly	Always
	0	1	2	3	4	5

A server loves being around other people because this provides him with more opportunities for service. He likes having guests and showing hospitality. The server is the first one to volunteer his home for a fellowship. He'll say, "Why don't you come to our house? We'd love to have you over." That's the way he is. He just wants to serve others.

You don't need the personality of a server in order to enjoy spending time with people. We are all called to extend hospitality to one another, but servers are especially bent in this direction; they just love being around people. They like working with people while they listen to others interact. They love expressing themselves to others. They love family gatherings with lots of children and grandchildren—the more the merrier.

▶ **A server loves being around people.**

Rate yourself:	Never	Seldom	Sometimes	Usually	Mostly	Always
	0	1	2	3	4	5

A server prefers working on immediate goals rather than long-range goals. She likes to see a task finished. There is one sure way to frustrate a server. Give her a project that will take five years. She likes to do a job and see it completed, but she doesn't like projects that have no end.

Gifted for Life's Journey

A server will stick to a task until it is accomplished because he has an incredible drive to finish what he starts. He is the most dependable person imaginable.

If you give him a short-term project, you can count on that assignment being completed. One reason long-range projects are so frustrating to him is because, not only does he want to finish it, but he wants to do it well.

Let me tell you where the server has a problem. The Christian life is not a short sprint but is a long-term endurance test, and a server can become frustrated. My advice to a server is to take life one day at a time. He may feel overwhelmed when he faces a long lasting tragedy, but if he can break that hardship down into bite-sized chunks, then he will be able to endure it.

Paul's theme in 1 Timothy is endurance. He repeatedly encourages Timothy to stick with it, hang in there, and endure to the end. In 1 Timothy 4:16, Paul tells Timothy, "Take heed to yourself and to the doctrine. Continue in them; for in doing this, you will save both yourself and those who hear you."

▶ **A server prefers working on immediate goals rather than long-range goals.**

Rate yourself:	Never	Seldom	Sometimes	Usually	Mostly	Always
	0	1	2	3	4	5

Day Four

A server feels inadequate as a leader but readily supports those who are in leadership. Don't ask a server to lead a group from point *A* to point *B*. The server does not like to be in a leadership role. It can create tremendous tension in a marriage when a husband is gifted in the area of service and loves doing practical things, but his wife expects him to be a leader in their church.

You can be just as godly working behind the scenes as you can be as a leader. God made followers as well as leaders so that they could work together to accomplish a ministry.

A server doesn't function well in a management position because he doesn't know how to delegate tasks to others. He spends the entire time thinking, "I could be doing that. Why did I ask her to do it?" He feels guilty if he is not doing something with his hands. More often than not, he will just do the task himself because he is a hands-on person.

Servers are the glue that holds the church together. If we were all prophets or administrators, we would be in a mess because everyone would be trying to

The Gift of Service

lead, and no one would be getting anything accomplished. Servers are the ones who get the job done.

For example, a server makes a great Sunday school teacher in a small class. He doesn't necessarily feel comfortable getting up in front of a group, and he feels inadequate in regard to his teaching ability, but because he is constantly checking up on the people in his class, he has an ability to build a close-knit class fellowship.

There is something about being around a server that will absolutely uplift you. He has a drive to serve and a desire to follow. He is a strong supporter of those in leadership positions. He will say something like, "Pastor, we love you and we're with you all the way." The server has the capacity to do whatever is necessary to assist and stand behind those in leadership.

▶ **A server feels inadequate as a leader but readily supports those who are in leadership.**

Rate yourself:	Never	Seldom	Sometimes	Usually	Mostly	Always
	0	1	2	3	4	5

A server operates at a high energy level. The server usually has three speeds—fast, faster, and fastest. His energy seems to be unlimited. Often, he gets by on less sleep than the average person. A server who operates in the Spirit appears to be tireless because he relies on the Lord's ability to work through him. When the server gets in the flesh however, he loses the energy that God has built into him and becomes lazy. He may also begin to look inward at himself.

Timothy was an enthusiastic and energetic young man. Paul told him in 1 Timothy 4:12-13, "Let no one despise your youth, but be an example to the believers in word, in conduct, in love, in spirit, in faith, in purity. Till I come, give attention to reading, to exhortation, to doctrine." Paul reminded Timothy to maintain his energetic, youthful approach to ministry and to give attention to these things.

▶ **A server operates at a high energy level.**

Rate yourself:	Never	Seldom	Sometimes	Usually	Mostly	Always
	0	1	2	3	4	5

Gifted for Life's Journey

Your Score on the Gift of Service

Take a few moments now to look back and copy your scores for this week. Add up your total points for the gift of service at the bottom of the page.

_____ Servers quickly spot practical needs and feel compelled to meet those needs in a swift, meticulous manner.

_____ Servers derive joy and a sense of purpose in serving others beyond the expected.

_____ Servers tend to sacrifice their own needs, even personal health, to serve others.

_____ Servers have difficulty saying "no" to requests for help.

_____ Servers enjoy manual projects that combine attention to detail with a remarkable memory.

_____ Servers need communication of specific instructions before service is rendered and appreciation afterward.

_____ Servers love to be around other people.

_____ Servers prefer working on immediate goals rather than long-range goals.

_____ Servers feel inadequate as a leader but readily supports those who are in leadership.

_____ Servers operate at a high energy level.

_____ **Total Points**

42

The Gift of Service

Day Five

The Problems of the Gift of Service

The server may be misunderstood in several ways. His desire to meet needs may be interpreted as a desire to promote himself. He doesn't check with a committee or follow the right channels. A server doesn't like red tape or bureaucracy or being told that he can't do something. He just rolls up his sleeves and does whatever needs to be done. This can be interpreted as trying to usurp authority, but he is simply trying to do the work that he feels compelled to do.

A server needs to know that his ministry is effective by having appreciation expressed to him. This can be misinterpreted as a desire to be praised. If he is in the flesh, a server will work for the approval of people rather than the approval of God. One of the pitfalls for a server is to want people to be pleased with him rather than disappoint them. He has to maintain a constant spiritual check on himself to insure that he is serving for the benefit of God alone and according to His will.

There will be times when a server feels compelled to meet so many needs that he simply can't meet them all. He will be disappointed in himself and will struggle with a tremendous amount of guilt because he feels burdened to meet every need. A server may be misunderstood because his drive to accomplish a task may be seen as being insensitive to others.

The server often offends people because he is so driven to serve that he finds it hard to accept being served by others. It is difficult for him to accept a gift. If he receives an anonymous gift, he will feel frustrated if he can't find out who it is so that he can do something nice for that person. The server must learn how to receive and to be blessed.

The server sees needs before anyone else. Many times he will move too soon to meet a need, and the other person is offended because he didn't even realize he had a need. The person may understand later on that the server was right all along. I've seen this happen with grandparents. They think they know what is best for their grandchildren, but the mother and father say, "Would you please let us take care of our own children!" That grandparent feels compelled to meet the need anyway, and in the process, she may cause friction in the family.

A server believes everyone ought to be constantly doing something to meet a need, and he may seem judgmental of those who are not. One of the toughest things for a server to do is to wait for God to work because he is driven to take care of needs.

Gifted for Life's Journey

His reaction when a need is revealed is often comical. A prophet sees someone in need and thinks, "That's what he gets for being out of God's will." A giver says, "Let's take up a collection to help him through this tough time." A teacher says, "Let's teach him what to do." But a server will say, "Let's just go take care of his need!" A server in the Spirit will recognize that God has a purpose for each type of personality.

The Practice of the Gift of Service

A Server in the Spirit

Now we will look at signs to know when a server is operating in God's will. When the following characteristics are evident, that person is living by the power of the Holy Spirit.

Alertness
He looks for needs that other people have.

Hospitality
He loves to be around people and moves quickly to meet their needs.

Generosity
The server gives freely of himself, his time, his talent, and his money.

Availability
You can call on a server any time, day or night, and He will be there in an instant.

Flexibility
He can change directions easily in order to go wherever the need is greatest.

The Gift of Service

Endurance
A server will get the job done although he prefers not to have a long-range project.

Joy
It is his delight to meet others' needs.

A Server in the Flesh

There are also seven things that indicate when a server is operating in the flesh. These are warning signs that a server is no longer in God's will.

Insensitivity
He loses the capacity to see the needs of others and becomes too focused on himself. When a server gets in the flesh, he can create discord in a church. He can lose his sensitivity to the Holy Spirit's ability to show him the needs that should be met.

Seclusion
The server stops serving and becomes isolated and lonely when he is trapped in the flesh. He may retreat into his own world because of a crisis or a hurt, and he becomes miserable and unfulfilled.

Stinginess
He doesn't want to have any part in giving or even to hear about it.

Detachment
You will hear him say, "Leave me alone!" He doesn't want to talk about problems or work through them because he is controlled by the flesh.

Rigidity
He becomes inflexible. You may hear him say, "Don't tell me what to do. I'll do it my own way. I can do this quite well without you."

Resignation

You will hear a server in the flesh say, "I quit." Whenever I hear that a server has resigned a position of service that was fulfilling to him, then I know something is wrong spiritually in his life or in his family.

Frustration

When a server begins to speak words of self-pity like, "Nobody appreciates all that I do," he is controlled by the flesh, because he is more focused on himself rather than on meeting other people's needs. A server is a delightful person when he is in the Spirit, but he is a monster in the flesh.

Timothy's Example

Paul often counted on Timothy to look after the people and specific needs that concerned him. He trusted Timothy to help him with the important details of the ministry. Paul also reminded Timothy not to over extend himself or become entangled with the routine activities of life. Knowing it would be a challenge for Timothy to endure the life-long race as a Christian, Paul encouraged him to remain focused on those things that were truly important.

Dealing With a Server as a Child

If you have a child who is bent in this direction, you will rarely need to ask him to clean up his room because he will do it on his own. He will keep his surroundings neat and orderly.

Don't overload a child who has this gift with several tasks at once. Just give him one project at a time. When he finishes it, tell him how much you appreciate him for what he did, and then give him the next project.

She is not likely to run for president of her class. Don't be disappointed because he does not receive tremendous accolades from his peers. It would be completely out of character for a person with the gift of service to seek those things. He will be much more comfortable in the background, letting others receive all the attention while he is busy with the tasks necessary to keep everything running smoothly. Remember that his role is just as important as those in the spotlight.

The Gift of Service

If being a server is not your particular personality, it is important to understand that God calls all of us to be servants. If you know that God has formed you in this direction, you have a responsibility to demonstrate the Spirit of Christ in meeting the needs of others so that those of us who are not gifted in this area will understand what it means to have a servant's heart. I have learned to serve by watching those who are bent in this direction.

If you are a servant operating in the flesh, refocus your attention and begin to operate on the basis of the Spirit. Reach out to meet the needs of others because that is what Jesus did, and He is our best example.

Week Four

The Gift of Teaching

...he who teaches, in teaching... Romans 12:7b

Day One

This week we will look at the third spiritual gift listed in Romans 12, the gift of teaching. There is a common misconception that you must have the gift of teaching in order to teach a Bible class. This is no truer than thinking you must have the gift of giving to support the ministry of your church through your tithes and offerings, or the gift of evangelism to share Christ with others. Some people are gifted by God to give generously or to present the gospel with great effectiveness. Others are gifted to investigate and teach the truth.

A person who has the gift of teaching usually makes a poor children's teacher, since children are not interested in technical explanations and minute details. Rather, this person is usually best suited for teaching adult and college-age classes.

However, the person who has been gifted by God as a teacher is not limited only to teaching. In fact, the teacher may not necessarily enjoy teaching a class at all. There are many other roles he can fill in the body of the church, as we will see this week.

The Personality of the Teacher

A teacher believes that the discovery of truth is the foundation of all that is important. He wants to establish the truth in every situation he encounters—education, business, human relationships. He believes very strongly that truth is found in the Bible, and he may shy away from anything that is not specifically grounded in Scripture.

The prophet wants an accurate understanding of the Bible so that he can perceive God's will, and the server wants to understand the Bible so that he will know how to meet needs. But the teacher simply wants to understand.

The Gift of Teaching

The teacher isn't necessarily people-oriented, but he is information-oriented. He believes that the process of discovering the truth is as important as, or even more important than, communicating the truth to others.

I can always spot the teachers in a church because they come up after the service is over and say, "Pastor, where did you get that interpretation?" or, "How do you see that in this passage of Scripture?" Sometimes a person who is not gifted as a teacher himself will be offended.

When a person with this gift is controlled by the flesh, he can find himself challenging his own pastor, saying, "Look, you are not applying this Scripture accurately," or, "You are not emphasizing this passage correctly." He is driven to uncover the truth and believes truth is the foundation of everything else.

Luke 1:1-4 gives us a better picture of a teacher than that found in any textbook. Luke says, "Inasmuch as many have taken in hand to set in order a narrative of those things which have been fulfilled among us...it seemed good to me also, having had perfect understanding of all things from the very first, to write to you an orderly account, most excellent Theophilus, that you may know the certainty of those things in which you were instructed." Luke is saying, in essence, "A lot of other people have written about this, but I've done my research and I'm going to tell you the truth because I understand it perfectly."

A teacher may seem egotistical to others, but Luke *did* know what he was talking about. Luke has details in his gospel that aren't found anywhere else because his teaching gift allowed him to record the events exactly as they happened.

▶ **A teacher believes that the discovery of truth is the foundation of all that is important.**

Rate yourself:	Never	Seldom	Sometimes	Usually	Mostly	Always
	0	1	2	3	4	5

A teacher delights in doing research and study. A person with this talent would rather study than do anything else. He usually has shelves full of books. He likes to dig into minute details of Scripture, searching to find the Greek or Hebrew meaning of a particular word. He is usually intelligent and makes good grades in school. His mind is like a sponge, and he has a great memory. He has a large vocabulary and usually enjoys crossword puzzles and games like Scrabble® and Trivial Pursuit®.

Many times a person with this gift enjoys researching truth more than actually presenting it. Often, listening to a preacher or professor with this particular aptitude is as boring as watching paint dry. I'm sure you remember a

Gifted for Life's Journey

brilliant professor or teacher in school. You knew that he was very learned and that he worked hard at teaching, but it would be all you could do to stay awake in his class. A teacher can become so enamored with the process of discovery that it may be difficult for him to present the truth in an interesting way.

▶ **A teacher delights in doing research and study.**

Rate yourself:	Never	Seldom	Sometimes	Usually	Mostly	Always
	0	1	2	3	4	5

Day Two

A teacher presents truth in a systematic manner. A teacher seems to speak in outline form. You can see that his mind works in a systematic fashion and that everything is compartmentalized. An instructor who has the gift of exhortation is great to listen to because he tells stories with gusto. But when he finishes, you won't have a single note written down or remember exactly what he said. You'll just know you enjoyed being in his class.

With one whose gift is teaching, however, you may not enjoy listening to him, but you will finish with a page full of notes. Everything will be in an orderly sequence that can be easily understood, and when you read your notes later, you will think, "That's really good—that's true."

Luke 1:3 says, "It seemed good to me also, having had a perfect understanding of all things from the every first, to write to you an orderly account...." And he did! Luke presented the life of Jesus very systematically, beginning with His birth and continuing through the crucifixion and resurrection. Luke then went on to tell his readers about the establishment of the early church. He had the ability to put in order and then accurately pass on information.

▶ **A teacher presents truth in a systematic manner.**

Rate yourself:	Never	Seldom	Sometimes	Usually	Mostly	Always
	0	1	2	3	4	5

A teacher evaluates all ideas by what he knows to be true. Teachers are driven to investigate the facts. They compare what a person says with what they

The Gift of Teaching

know to be true. They will ask a million questions, and they will investigate everything thoroughly; they want to know the truth.

They are very important to the church because they are constantly bringing us back to the Word. They will say, "Yes, I understand how you feel, and I know your experience, but what does the Bible say?"

You won't find many teachers in a cult or in a movement that is based on experience or emotion. They want to be grounded in the truth. Consequently, those who have this gift have difficulty walking by faith because they like to know everything in advance. They want things to be written out and explained to them in detail.

Teachers have a check and balance system that always brings them back to the foundation of the truth. They may get off base for a while, but if they continue to operate in the Spirit, they will come back.

When I was in college, my wife and I really wanted to find the truth for ourselves. We became involved for about two years in a cult called The Way International. The members made us feel accepted, but there was always a gnawing in my spirit that said, "Something isn't quite right here."

Although we were studying the Bible in this group, I saw that they taught some things that didn't measure up when I tested their teachings against the truth. The thing that clinched it for me was when the leader of the cult wrote a book entitled, *Jesus Christ is Not God.* We left that cult immediately and joined a biblically sound church.

Luke, when writing about Jesus and the birth of the church, stated he had "perfect understanding of all things." The Greek word for *understanding* can also be translated as *investigated.* Luke's careful investigation yielded the truth that he presented.

▶ **A teacher evaluates all ideas by what he knows to be true.**

Rate yourself:	Never	Seldom	Sometimes	Usually	Mostly	Always
	0	1	2	3	4	5

A teacher expresses an interest in the factual basis of what others have to say. He will ask a lot of questions. They are the ones who ask, "Where did you get your information? Are you sure it is accurate? How did you arrive at that conclusion?" You had better check out everything you have to say before you address a group of teachers.

Luke said that others had written about the events that had taken place, but he had examined the facts and put together an orderly presentation from beginning to end.

Gifted for Life's Journey

▶A teacher expresses an interest in the factual basis of what others have to say.

Rate yourself:	Never	Seldom	Sometimes	Usually	Mostly	Always
	0	1	2	3	4	5

Day Three

A teacher emphasizes accuracy down to the smallest detail. He doesn't care what you think; he just wants to know the facts. That is the reason he asks so many questions. A person with this gift is upset when a passage of Scripture is used out of context or misinterpreted. He will immediately recognize it, and you can almost see his skin crawling.

He wants correctness. That is why, in Luke 4:38, Luke didn't just say Peter's mother-in-law was ill. He said she was sick with a high fever. Luke was precise in his descriptions.

▶A teacher emphasizes accuracy to the most minute detail.

Rate yourself:	Never	Seldom	Sometimes	Usually	Mostly	Always
	0	1	2	3	4	5

A teacher is alert to spot details and facets of a situation unnoticed by others. She may discuss a familiar passage of Scripture and bring out things that you never saw before. It is good to have a doctor or an attorney who has this gift, because he will pursue every conceivable avenue and spot details others might miss.

I love to serve on a team with someone gifted as a teacher. Others will be talking all around an issue, but he will be quietly listening. He will finally say one thing, and it will be like an arrow shot right to the heart of the issue. Teachers are good problem solvers because they study the details and make an assessment accordingly.

The Gift of Teaching

▶ **A teacher is alert to spot details and facets of a situation unnoticed by others.**

Rate yourself:	Never	Seldom	Sometimes	Usually	Mostly	Always
	0	1	2	3	4	5

A teacher listens carefully to others before offering opinions. A person gifted as a teacher is not impulsive. He will weigh facts very carefully and think things through before acting. Many times he will appear wiser than he really is because he is so careful in his deliberations. He is a good listener, but don't expect him to offer sympathy or consolation. His analytical mind eschews emotions, preferring to concentrate on the information instead.

▶ **A teacher listens carefully to others before offering opinions.**

Rate yourself:	Never	Seldom	Sometimes	Usually	Mostly	Always
	0	1	2	3	4	5

Day Four

A teacher has a small, select group of friends. They are not generally known as people persons. They don't make good politicians because they're not good at shaking hands and kissing babies. You won't find them at the center of a group of people, leading in an animated conversation. Normally, they don't like large social gatherings and prefer smaller, more intimate settings. They enjoy talking, but want the conversation to be meaningful, not just a lot of silly chatter. They usually have only one or two good friends. Many times they are loners and are described as aloof.

Often they have built emotional walls around themselves to avoid being hurt by others. I have counseled people with this gift who grew up in very abusive situations, yet they've emerged virtually unscathed. This is because other people aren't as important to them as the information they can gather from a situation, even if that situation is their own painful experience.

Luke wrote the books of Luke and Acts to one person, his friend Theophilus. Paul wrote his letters to various churches and individuals, but Luke did all of the research and expended all of his effort to write to just one person. If

Gifted for Life's Journey

it had not been for Luke's writings, we would not have known what it was like in the beginning of the early church. But he was moved by the Holy Spirit to write all of that to Theophilus because Luke had the gift of teaching.

▶ **A teacher has a small, select group of friends.**

Rate yourself:	Never	Seldom	Sometimes	Usually	Mostly	Always
	0	1	2	3	4	5

A teacher exercises self-discipline and endurance with consistency. They usually have no problem setting personal goals and sticking with them. They don't give up or quit easily. When in the Spirit, they are the most emotionally stable of all the gifts. They are very analytical, so they are a good choice to help solve dilemmas or conflicts and they are good committee or group leaders.

When Paul was in prison and everyone else had abandoned him, he wrote, "Only Luke is with me (2 Timothy 4:11)." Luke stuck by him when everyone else fell by the wayside. His gift as a teacher enabled him to have the staying power and steadiness to remain by Paul's side when others had backed away.

A teacher exercises self-discipline and endurance with consistency.

Rate yourself:	Never	Seldom	Sometimes	Usually	Mostly	Always
	0	1	2	3	4	5

The Gift of Teaching

Your Score on the Gift of Teaching

Take a few moments now to look back and copy your scores for this week. Add up your total points for the gift of teaching at the bottom of the page.

_____ A teacher believes the discovery of truth is the foundation of all that is important.

_____ A teacher delights in doing research and study.

_____ A teacher presents truth in a systematic manner.

_____ A teacher evaluates all ideas by what he knows to be true.

_____ A teacher expresses an interest in the factual basis of what others have to say.

_____ A teacher emphasizes accuracy to the most minute detail.

_____ A teacher is alert to spot details and facets of a situation not noticed by others.

_____ A teacher listens carefully to others before offering an opinion.

_____ A teacher has a small, select group of friends.

_____ A teacher exercises self-discipline and endurance with consistency.

_____ **Total Points**

Day Five

The Problems of the Gift of Teacher

The gift of teaching can bring with it numerous problems. The person who has this gift may lack warmth. He knows a lot, but he may also have a know-it-all attitude if he has not dealt with the issue of pride in his life. He must be willing to humble himself and realize that he can't gain all the necessary knowledge through his own research.

Another problem I have noticed is that teachers tend to look down on the practical wisdom of others that has been learned through life experiences. If someone lacks qualifications and degrees, then a teacher may not think he is credible. Be wary of this tendency if you have the personality of a teacher.

Teachers also tend to forget that Proverbs 3:5 says, "Trust in the Lord with all your heart, and lean not on your own understanding." Teachers want to understand everything—to reason everything out. If they can't understand it, then they may become upset and withdraw into their world of research.

Teachers are easily distracted. They may start looking up *electricity* in the encyclopedia and end up reading about *eels* and *Edison* and *ecology* because they are so interested in what they are learning at the moment. They have loads of half-read books and a closet full of half-finished projects because it is so easy to lose their focus and be drawn away into other areas that interest them.

The Practice of the Gift of Teacher

A Teacher in the Spirit

Following are seven ways to tell if a teacher is operating in the Spirit.

Discipline
They will exhibit a great degree of self-control. They are not lazy because they are driven to study and investigate matters.

Thoroughness
Their work is impeccable, and they leave no loose ends. Because of this, others also have confidence in a teacher's abilities.

Reverence
They have respect for God's Word and for the truth. The more they learn, the more humble they become.

Patience
They could not spend so much time in study if they did not have patience. Attention to detail could only be accomplished with much patience.

Dependability
They desire to be a dependable resource that others will be able to rely on.

Security
They know what they are talking about because they have spent the necessary time to research the topic, and they are confident in what they are sharing.

Joy
A teacher, who has the capacity and the time necessary to glean the truth and then teach it to others, is literally overflowing with joy.

A Teacher in the Flesh

There are also seven words that are evidence that a teacher is walking in the flesh.

Self-indulgence
They become lazy and have no discipline in their lives. They handle the Scripture carelessly and fail to maintain a sense of fulfillment in their research.

Inconsistency

They will act by their own impetus, not by the leading of the Holy Spirit. You will see them become sloppy in many areas of their lives including the way they take care of themselves.

Disrespect

They lose their respect for the truth. You will hear them say things in a challenging manner like, "What gives you the right to that opinion? Who do you think you are?"

Impatience

They are restless and impatient. They are mean-spirited and lose their temper easily.

Unreliability

They become unreliable and are no longer a dependable, faithful authority.

Anxiety

The self-image of a teacher is wrapped up in what he knows, and it suffers when he doesn't study. He loses his security and becomes anxious. He is emotionally charged, ready to explode, and given to extreme emotional swings or outbursts. He has low self-esteem and is anxious about everything around him because he is not using his gift.

Frustration

They experience frustration with others and with themselves because they are not fulfilling their God-given purpose in life.

Luke's Example

Luke is a wonderful example of a biblical person who had this particular talent. Using his giftedness as a teacher, he carefully gathered the facts about the birth and ministry of Jesus as well as the formation of the early church. He wrote his description of these events for his friend, Theophilus. We have them today as the two books of the Bible, Luke and Acts.

The Gift of Teaching

To whom do we look at Christmas to read the account of the birth of the Christ Child? We go to Luke because he had details that no other gospel writer included. That was his ministry—his place of service—because he had been gifted with the ability to organize and convey information.

Luke was also steadfast. He didn't abandon Paul in a crisis even though others had turned away.

Dealing With a Teacher as a Child

A child who has this gift may be reclusive, preferring to spend time in her room rather than with friends. Other kids will often identify him as a nerd because he likes books and computers more than people. He may be so persistent with his questions that he will appear to be rude to adults. He is motivated to keep on inquiring so that he can validate the truth. This is the child who is always asking "why?"

While this child is young, do not discourage the questions that are asked. It may be irritating at times, but it will bear fruit in the life of your child if you do not squelch their inquisitive nature. As they grow older, train them to research their own answers.

Do the things we covered this week describe you? God made you as a unique individual so that you could fulfill the role that He has for you. He gifted some people as teachers so that you and I can learn from them.

Take my advice and begin faithfully using your gift for the good of all concerned, including yourself. Begin by prayerfully asking the Lord to show you His truth, then study His Word to discover the truth for yourself.

Finally, find a way in which you can pass this truth on to others. Only by using your gift, will you ever feel useful and fulfilled. God gave you a unique gift because He loves you, so by all means, start using it.

The worst thing you could do is sit back and refuse to allow God to use you. You would be saying, "God, I can handle this myself." Well, you can't! It is a sad thing to be made in the image of God and yet fail to reach the potential that God knows you could achieve.

Week Five

The Gift of Exhortation

...he who exhorts, in exhortation; Romans 12:8a

Day One

The word for exhortation in Romans 12 is the Greek word *paracletos*, which literally means to come alongside. Jesus used the same word in John 16:7, when He said, "Nevertheless I tell you the truth. It is to your advantage that I go away; for if I do not go away, the Helper will not come to you; but if I depart, I will send Him to you."

The Helper Jesus referred to in this verse is the Holy Spirit, the One who was to come alongside the disciples and encourage them in their mission. Jesus told them that if He did not go away, the Holy Spirit would not come to them; so therefore it was better for them if He did leave. The role of the Holy Spirit is to inhabit each believer with the full presence of the living God, thereby strengthening and encouraging them.

The exhorter's job is similar to that of the Holy Spirit: to encourage and help his fellow Christians grow to maturity, to give them strength for the tasks ahead, and to be the cheerleader of the church. I firmly believe that every believer should have an exhorter as a personal friend because the exhorter can help the believer realize his full potential, just as the Holy Spirit does when He comes alongside us.

The exhorter will exhibit several distinct and unique personality traits. You can learn to recognize an exhorter by his attitudes and actions.

The Personality of the Exhorter

First, an exhorter encourages others to spiritual maturity. The exhorter wants every believer to have a full and meaningful life; to be fulfilled and to live up to his potential. The greatest joy that an exhorter has is in encouraging or building up people. He is not interested in activities or programs. He wants to see people challenged and to achieve their personal best.

The Gift of Exhortation

You don't have to look far for a biblical example of a person who has the gift of encouragement, or exhortation. Paul wrote many of the books of the New Testament as letters of encouragement to other believers. He wanted them to be challenged and changed, so they could achieve the potential with which God had created them.

One such example is in Colossians 1:28. Speaking of Jesus, Paul says, "Him we preach, warning every man and teaching every man in all wisdom, that we may present every man perfect in Christ Jesus." The word *perfect* in the Greek means mature. In other words, Paul preached about Jesus because he wanted to see everyone grow up and mature in Him.

▶ **An exhorter encourages others to spiritual maturity.**

Rate yourself:	Never	Seldom	Sometimes	Usually	Mostly	Always
	0	1	2	3	4	5

An exhorter perceives where a person is in his maturing process and visualizes his potential for growth. She will ask a lot of questions, and you may feel that she is a little too nosy. However, she is only trying to find out where you are spiritually so she can help you achieve your God-given potential.

To an exhorter, everyone is in the process of maturing in Christ, and he wants every member of the body of Christ to function together as a unit. Whether in a group or individually, an exhorter will be able to see your potential. He may recognize something in you that you never thought of, and he will usually be right. He can visualize what you could accomplish if God had control of your life.

Exhorters are faith-oriented people. I admire those with this gift because they can look ahead with a sense of vision, and encourage others to join them to accomplish a goal. They are always looking for ways to help others become their very best, and they are willing to begin wherever necessary.

That was Paul's motivation when he said in 1 Corinthians 3:1, "And I, brethren, could not speak to you as to spiritual people but as to carnal, as to babes in Christ." Paul knew not only where they were in their spiritual walk, but also where they could go. He was willing to start with them in their spiritual immaturity and lead them to the point of maturity. He wanted to help them grow up in Christ.

▶**An exhorter perceives where a person is in his maturing process and visualizes his potential for growth.**

Rate yourself:	Never	Seldom	Sometimes	Usually	Mostly	Always
	0	1	2	3	4	5

Gifted for Life's Journey

Day Two

An exhorter prescribes definite steps of action to take a person from where he is to where he needs to be. They are enormously gifted with a capability for giving practical and helpful advice. If you want guidance, ask an exhorter. He will quickly evaluate where you are and where you are going, then he will give you the steps to get there. People seek them out for guidance, and they make great counselors, if they will stay in the Spirit rather than in the flesh.

One of the best things you can do is to find an exhorter to act as your counselor. Sit down with him and tell him, "Here is where I am and there is where I need to be. How do I get there?" God may speak to you through him. You will be surprised what you can learn about God's direction for your life.

Paul's letters have a doctrinal section first, and then a second practical section. They are filled with step-by-step processes to take you from where you are to where you need to be.

► **An exhorter prescribes definite steps of action to take a person from where he is to where he needs to be.**

Rate yourself:	Never	Seldom	Sometimes	Usually	Mostly	Always
	0	1	2	3	4	5

An exhorter expects to see a visible response to their prescribed steps. They don't like e-mail or other impersonal methods of communication. They want to be a part of people's lives and to interact with others on a personal level. They want to see a reaction when they offer advice.

When you speak to an exhorter, he will be watching the way you express yourself through your body language and your facial expressions. He will soak up everything about you. An exhorter who is anointed with the Spirit of God will make you feel like you are the most important person in the world.

He will rivet his attention on you, and you will be amazed that he is so interested in you. Frequently an exhorter, while he is watching and listening to you, is not necessarily sympathizing with you. His motivation is to formulate ways he can help you.

An exhorter is frustrated when he gives advice which is ignored. He sees where a person is, but he also sees where he can go, and he is disheartened if you come back a week later and you have not moved from point *A* to point *B*. He wants to see a visible response; to see you making correct decisions and to know

62

The Gift of Exhortation

that he has had an impact on your life. He wants to help you, to encounter you personally, give advice on how to proceed, and see that you have heeded his advice.

Paul was always eager to return to the churches he had established so that he could see those believers face to face and encourage them. One of the greatest pains in Paul's life happened in Thessalonica. He stayed there three weeks, started a church, and was forced to leave by some of the Jews who opposed him.

He couldn't go back there because he was under the threat of death, but he wrote to the church in 1 Thessalonians 2:17, "But we, brethren, having been taken away from you for a short time in presence, not in heart, endeavored more eagerly to see your face with great desire." An exhorter is motivated to touch a person's life and see that person achieving his full potential.

▶An exhorter expects to see a visible response to the prescribed steps.

Rate yourself:	Never	Seldom	Sometimes	Usually	Mostly	Always
	0	1	2	3	4	5

An exhorter identifies easily with people and effectively communicates a message of unity among diverse groups. People enjoy being around exhorters. They are good communicators, so they do well in jobs that require giftedness in speech. They make good mediators and can help reconcile people who are in disagreement with each other.

They can easily identify with a wide array of groups with diverse interests and can usually work effectively to promote harmony. Exhorters can walk into a tense situation and soon have everyone working together.

Take, for example, a family fight. A prophet marches in and says, "Look, this is how it is going to be. If you don't like it, there's the door." A mercy-giver says, "Oh, I know you are hurting, and I hurt with you."

An exhorter wades into the middle of a situation, rolls up his sleeves, and says, "Let's get together and work this out." He actually enjoys it. He has the ability to create unity out of a stressful situation.

Paul said in Philippians 2:2, "Fulfill my joy by being like-minded, having the same love, being of one accord, of one mind." Paul emphasized unity and bringing people together.

▶ An exhorter identifies easily with people and effectively communicates a message of unity among diverse groups.

Rate yourself:	Never	Seldom	Sometimes	Usually	Mostly	Always
	0	1	2	3	4	5

Gifted for Life's Journey

Day Three

An exhorter finds truth in practical experiences and then validates it with Scripture. Life is full of lessons and insights to exhorters. They get really fired up about touching lives. Experience is their primary teacher. When they see something happen, they immediately begin to draw lessons from that experience.

This can also be a real pitfall for exhorters. They can fall into a heretical group because of an experience they've had. They can abandon the doctrinal truth of the Scripture and can embrace ideas and philosophies that are not scriptural.

Don't tell an exhorter, "That isn't what the Word of God says." He will reply, "Yes, but that's what I've experienced." An exhorter usually uses experience as his test of truth, and if he is not careful, he will elevate his own experience above what the Word of God says. When he does that, he has stepped over the line into sin.

An exhorter always wants his experience to become a practical lesson for others. He doesn't want small talk or chit chat, but he wants what is said to be meaningful.

It is interesting to see the way people with different personalities will listen to a sermon. For example, a prophet will listen and ask himself, "What is God saying?" A server will listen to a sermon and think, "What can I do about this?" The teacher will be asking, "Is this accurate? Did he get his facts right?" The exhorter, on the other hand, hears a sermon and thinks, "How can I apply this? Can I communicate this to someone else?"

Reasoning is extremely important to exhorters. Paul's most convincing arguments in the Scripture were drawn from his experience. In Acts 18:4 we are told that "he reasoned in the synagogue every Sabbath, and persuaded both Jews and Greeks."

In Acts 17, Paul began witnessing to the Athenians by describing the unknown god to whom they had built a statue. Paul was applying his gift as an exhorter by understanding his audience's situation and using it as a starting point for teaching them about the one true God.

▶ **An exhorter finds truth in practical experiences and then validates it with Scripture.**

Rate yourself:	Never	Seldom	Sometimes	Usually	Mostly	Always
	0	1	2	3	4	5

64

The Gift of Exhortation

An exhorter views personal trials as opportunities for spiritual growth. The word impossible is not in an exhorter's vocabulary. They see opportunities, not obstacles; challenges, not trials; possibilities, not problems. They stay focused on the solution rather than the problem; they keep their eyes on Jesus. They firmly believe Romans 8:28, "All things work together for good to those who love God, to those who are the called according to His purpose." When bad things happen, they believe there is a positive reason for it and look for ways to use it to encourage others. No matter how difficult a situation is, they seek to use suffering as a means to bring them closer to God.

That is much different from the way a person with the gift of mercy will approach suffering. Mercy-givers wipe away the tears and say, "I love you, let me hold you." An exhorter sees suffering and says, "God will turn everything around and make this a positive thing in your life. Remember that God is working on you." They see suffering as a means to an end, which is greater maturity for you.

Even Paul, in 2 Corinthians 12:8-10, pleaded with the Lord three times to remove his thorn in the flesh. God reminded him, "My grace is sufficient for you." Then Paul said, "I take pleasure in infirmities...for when I am weak, then I am strong." Paul understood that he needed to begin to operate in the power of the Spirit.

► **An exhorter views personal trials as opportunities for spiritual growth.**

Rate yourself:	Never	Seldom	Sometimes	Usually	Mostly	Always
	0	1	2	3	4	5

An exhorter acts with decisiveness and then moves on without regret. Exhorters can make decisions in a snap. They are action oriented people and believe life is too short to be indecisive. Their thinking is, "Let's decide and then move on."

Their decisions are usually right on target if their minds are saturated with the truth of God and they are following God's direction. Their philosophy is, "If I do something wrong, God will correct me later. If I suffer for it, I can use that to encourage someone else." They have a tremendously practical side.

They don't, however, like difficulties with other people and will try to resolve any strained relationships they may experience. If necessary, they are even willing to take the blame for something they didn't do in order to restore a relationship. They can't stand having anyone angry with them.

Paul said in Philippians 3:17, "Brethren, join in following my example, and note those who so walk, as you have us for a pattern." Notice Paul's decisiveness. He means, "Come on, imitate me and those of us who are walking with Jesus. Just move out for God."

Gifted for Life's Journey

▶ **An exhorter acts with decisiveness and then moves on without regret.**

Rate yourself:	Never	Seldom	Sometimes	Usually	Mostly	Always
	0	1	2	3	4	5

Day Four

An exhorter performs all tasks with thoroughness and endurance. You won't find an exhorter leaving anything unfinished. They will usually finish the letters they start and work overtime to accomplish projects and assignments. They don't mind burning the midnight oil.

There is one situation, however, where an exhorter will tend to give up. If a person that he is trying to help refuses to follow his advice, an exhorter will finally say, "Sorry, I can't help you." Success, to an exhorter, is measured by how much he can help someone. If a person refuses his help, he feels that there is nothing else he can do for them. Exhorters, with that one exception, are noted for their endurance.

Paul said in 2 Timothy 4:7, "I have fought the good fight, I have finished the race, I have kept the faith." This is an example of an exhorter's willingness to stay on track and finish what he starts.

▶ **An exhorter performs all tasks with thoroughness and endurance.**

Rate yourself:	Never	Seldom	Sometimes	Usually	Mostly	Always
	0	1	2	3	4	5

An exhorter has high expectations for himself and for others. Exhorters feel that few people really live up to their potential, so they are always encouraging people to stretch beyond their comfort zone. They believe that when you get beyond your own capacity, then you really begin to determine the potential God has for you.

Exhorters make terrible pew warmers. I guess that is one reason I like them so much; because they have to be active and doing something all the time. They need to be involved in helping others. It frustrates them not to be doing something—not to be making a difference in people's lives.

Paul expected a great deal of himself and had no problem expecting the same of others. In Philippians 4:9 he said, "The things which you learned and

66

The Gift of Exhortation

received and heard and saw in me, these do, and the God of peace will be with you." In other words, "You've seen me do it, now you go out and do it." He had high expectations for himself and for others.

▶ **An exhorter has high expectations for himself and for others.**

Rate yourself:	Never	Seldom	Sometimes	Usually	Mostly	Always
	0	1	2	3	4	5

Gifted for Life's Journey

Your Score on the Gift of Exhortation

Take time now to look back and copy your scores for this week. Add up your total points for the gift of exhortation at the bottom of the page.

_____ An exhorter encourages others to spiritual maturity.

_____ An exhorter perceives where a person is in his maturing process and visualizes his potential for growth.

_____ An exhorter prescribes definite steps of action to take a person from where he is to where he needs to be.

_____ An exhorter expects to see a visible response to the prescribed steps.

_____ An exhorter identifies easily with people and effectively communicates a message of unity among diverse groups.

_____ An exhorter finds truth in practical experiences and then validates it with Scripture.

_____ An exhorter views personal trials as opportunities for spiritual growth.

_____ An exhorter acts with decisiveness and then moves on without regret.

_____ An exhorter performs all tasks with thoroughness and endurance.

_____ An exhorter has high expectations for himself and others.

_____ **Total Points**

The Gift of Exhortation

| Day Five |

The Problems of the Gift of Exhortation

Let me show you how an exhorter can easily get in the flesh. He develops the mentality that he has all the answers and everyone else ought to listen to what he has to say. He believes that if people aren't listening to him, then something must be wrong with those people. Sometimes an exhorter will think, "I gave you three easy steps and you didn't follow them, so I can't help you." He sometimes forgets that it is not his responsibility to point people to these three easy steps, but rather to point them to God. If people encounter God, then He can change their heart.

You also have to be very careful about the fact that exhorters will seek truth from experience. The only real test for truth is the Word of God because that is where the absolutes are determined.

The Practice of the Gift of Exhortation

An Exhorter in the Spirit

Here are seven ways to tell if an exhorter is operating in the Spirit

Wisdom
When an exhorter is walking in the Spirit he knows and understands the Scripture.

Discernment
An exhorter has a tremendous capacity for seeing things as they really are. He knows how to help you move along as a believer. He understands just how to direct and guide you and how fast you need to go.

Faith
They see potential and believe God can get you there. They trust Him.

69

Love
They accept you as you are. They evaluate, but don't judge or accuse. They come alongside you and help, if you ask them.

Creativity
Exhorters have a tremendous capacity for discerning where people are spiritually, and then finding a creative way to touch their lives.

Enthusiasm
They are extremely positive. They are the cheerleaders. They'll say, "You can make it. Hang in there."

Joy
They have confidence in God, which brings them tremendous joy.

An Exhorter in the Flesh

In contrast, here are seven characteristics that are evidence that the exhorter is walking in the flesh.

Foolishness
They are prone to fall into the trap of believing in the truth of the moment, or whatever belief is currently popular. They can be easily misled into cults or other quasi-religious groups. They believe, if a particular theory has worked for others, then it can work for them.

Impulsiveness
They will immediately jump on issues and situations. When an exhorter is in the flesh, he is so gullible he will believe anything because he loses the capacity to discern the truth. He can be so critical he will say things without thinking like, "How did you get into this mess? What's wrong with you?"

Presumption
They presume upon God and demand things of Him. They don't trust and walk with God.

The Gift of Exhortation

Selfishness

When an exhorter isolates himself from people, you will hear him say things like, "Don't bother me. I've done all I know to do. Just leave me alone."

Everyone needs some reflective time alone with God to recharge his batteries, but when an exhorter decides he doesn't want to be with people and builds a wall around himself, he is operating in the flesh.

Generality

They lose their capacity for being creative in helping others achieve their potential. They treat people with disinterest and try to make everyone conform to their own ideas. They establish boundaries and expect everyone to adhere to them.

Apathy

They lose their enthusiasm and interest in others. They don't touch people or want to help others, and they become uncaring.

Frustration

It is sad to see an exhorter operating in the flesh because, in the process of his frustration, he loses touch with what God wants to do in his life.

Paul's Example

Paul's letters of encouragement in the New Testament challenge believers to mature into the people God intends for us to be. He spoke to those who had far to go and gave them step by step instructions to reach spiritual maturity. Paul longed to see them established and unified in the faith. He understood what it took to live a successful Christian life to the very end and didn't hesitate to urge others to follow his example.

Dealing With a Exhorter as a Child

You can tell if your child is an exhorter if he is bossy. He whisks into the room and tells the little brother, the big sister, and all the neighbor's kids what to do and how to do it. He just takes over and runs the show. If you aren't careful, that little exhorter can grow up to be a nagging, controlling person who makes everyone around him miserable.

It is important for those of you who are parents of an exhorter to teach your child to focus on God. The best thing you can do for your child is to continually direct him toward God. Otherwise he will become so self-confident that he develops a cocky attitude. He needs to draw his confidence from the Lord and from what He can do in his life, rather than from his own abilities.

Are you operating according to the joy of the Spirit of God, or are you operating in the flesh? It is such a waste when God creates you with so much potential and wants to work through you to accomplish His will, but you tell Him you would rather do it your own way. God's way is the best way. We must be willing to yield to the touch of His Spirit and allow Him to have His way in us.

Week Six

The Gift of Giving

...he who gives, with liberality; Romans 12:8b

Day One

Not everyone has the gift of giving, but we are all called to give. As 2 Corinthians 9:7 says, "So let each one give as he purposes in his heart, not grudgingly or of necessity; for God loves a cheerful giver." It does not say that only those who have the gift of giving are to give, but rather that each one, meaning *everyone*, is to give willingly and cheerfully to meet the needs of others.

There are some people, however, who are blessed with the ability and the desire to give above and beyond their means to do so. This gift is not limited to people who have great riches. In fact, more often than not, people with the gift of giving are not wealthy, but they act as a channel that God uses to distribute a great deal of the world's wealth.

One of the primary examples of this was George Mueller. He developed a tremendous burden for the orphans of London in the 1700s. He did not have the funds necessary to meet their needs, so he began to rely on prayer. At one time, George Mueller was the sole provider for over 2,050 orphans, along with the staff necessary to care for them. He would pray, "Lord, these are not mine: they are Yours; therefore I trust You to meet their needs." During his lifetime, millions of dollars passed through his hands to care for orphaned children, but George Mueller was never wealthy. When he died, he had just enough money to pay for his burial. What more does a person really need? The ministry he began continues today, some two hundred years later, and still conducts no financial campaigns. Its leaders just trust God to meet their needs. George Mueller had learned the secret of being a giver.

The giver is probably the least likely of anyone to know that he is distinctive by virtue of his gift. It is sometimes difficult to distinguish between a server and a giver because they share many of the same characteristics. Both can be either a leader or a follower, and they have an inherent love for the Word of God.

In Romans 12:8, Paul speaks of "he who gives, with liberality." The word *gives* in the Greek is *metadidomi* which means to share or impart. The giver never sees himself as giving up anything. He views himself as sharing what he has with others, and he does this with liberality.

Gifted for Life's Journey

This Greek word *haplotetes* literally means with sincerity or generosity. He loves to exercise his gift again and again and many times will do so over abundantly. Givers do not care about having a lot of money. They will share, not only their possessions and money, but also of themselves.

The Personality of the Giver

The first character trait to notice is that the giver is generous with money, possessions, time, energy, and love. He is often able to choose wise investments so that he has more to give. It seems that the more a giver has or receives, the more he gives. He receives abundant blessings in the process of his giving.

I love to watch a person with this gift as she shops. Most people look for a bargain so they can have more money to spend on themselves, but not a giver. A giver shops for the best bargain so that she will have more to share with someone else. They love to give things away. If you need a bed, he will give you his own bed. He knows that God blesses him in giving; then he learns to be more generous and gives even more away.

As an example, a young homemaker living on a tight budget wanted to express her gift of giving, so she took her Christmas card list and began to pray specifically for one person on her list each day. She wrote them a personal letter and made a bookmark with a Bible verse that God put on her heart especially for that person. In this way, she exemplified the giver's motto, "The best gift is to give yourself."

▶ **The giver is generous with money, possessions, time, energy, and love.**

Rate yourself:	Never	Seldom	Sometimes	Usually	Mostly	Always
	0	1	2	3	4	5

The giver derives pleasure from giving without recognition. Suppose there was a need for $10,000 for a special project in the church, and there was an announcement made asking for someone to start by giving the first $1,000. Then imagine someone stood and said, "I believe in this cause, and I will!" That would be great and exciting, but that person would not have the gift of giving because givers don't want other people to know when they give. They are not motivated by applause or by recognition. Many times a giver will go to extreme lengths to insure that others do not find out about their generous gifts. They just love to see God take their gift and use it for His glory.

There once was a man who noticed a teenager in his church who was very self-conscience about her protruding teeth. Her mother was recently widowed and

The Gift of Giving

could not afford to provide braces for her daughter. This man quietly went to an orthodontist in town, gave him $3,000, and asked him to take care of the girl's teeth, but to keep his identity a secret. The only reward he wanted was the joy of watching her smile blossom. That tells us he was blessed with the gift of giving.

Matthew is the only gospel writer who speaks of giving in secret, and that is a great indicator of what was in Matthew's heart. In Matthew 6:3-4 he says, "But when you do a charitable deed, do not let your left hand know what your right hand is doing that your charitable deed may be in secret; and your Father who sees in secret will Himself reward you openly."

► **The giver derives pleasure from giving without recognition.**

Rate yourself:

	Never	Seldom	Sometimes	Usually	Mostly	Always
	0	1	2	3	4	5

Day Two

The giver believes God is both the source and the motivation of giving. They see everything as belonging to God and coming from God, and they love to help Him distribute it. Many times they are uniquely blessed to earn a very good living, but they also find it easy to live by faith, trusting God to meet their needs. You cannot coerce a mature giver into giving. They will hear a television evangelist say, "If you don't send money to us, we will have to go off the air," and they will just change stations. They do not give out of guilt or because of high pressure tactics. They give because God put that particular ability in their lives.

Some interesting discussions result when a giver is married to a non-giver. The non-giver is thinking of the bills that must be paid, and the giver is thinking about the needs he can meet. He will say, "Don't worry, God will take care of us," and he is usually right. As long as a giver stays focused on God's will for his life, and meets only the needs that God directs him to meet, he will be a conduit to deliver God's blessings to others. It is wonderful to watch givers as they live their lives on the basis of faith. I learn so much from them because they operate in a realm of faith that is foreign to many Christians. They learn to trust God explicitly.

The person with the gift of giving must keep his priorities straight. Matthew 6:24 says, "No man can serve two masters; for either he will hate the one and love the other, or else he will be loyal to the one and despise the other. You cannot serve God and mammon." The giver must make sure he is serving God above all else.

They give themselves to prayer and evangelism. Some of the greatest soul winners are givers because they see salvation through Jesus Christ as the greatest

Gifted for Life's Journey

gift of all. They love to win someone to Jesus, and they trust God to use them to accomplish that goal.

A giver gives as though giving to God and not for his own credit. Jesus says He will return and search men's hearts to determine their motivation in giving. Matthew 25:40 says, "And the King will answer and say to them, 'Assuredly, I say to you, inasmuch as you did it to one of the least of these My brethren, you did it to Me."

▶ **The giver believes God is both the source and the motivation of giving.**

Rate yourself:	**Never**	**Seldom**	**Sometimes**	**Usually**	**Mostly**	**Always**
	0	**1**	**2**	**3**	**4**	**5**

The giver is thrilled to discover that a gift is an answer to prayer and can be used as a blessing to others. Givers give as prompted by the Holy Spirit. They are delighted when you respond to their gift by saying, "How did you know I needed this? I've been praying for this." That tells them they are in tune with the Holy Spirit. When they know that they are the tool by which God has met your need, they receive a special blessing from giving.

Givers will often be burdened to meet a specific need. They may come to their pastor and say, "I can't explain this, but I have a burden to give a certain person this money. Would you please see that they get it, but don't let anyone know where it came from?" Invariably, the recipient had been praying about a need for that exact amount. When a giver is in tune with the Holy Spirit, it is amazing how God works to reveal to him the needs of others.

Givers are prone to investigate a situation thoroughly. They want to make sure that their gift is properly used, and that they are truly being used by God to meet a need. They will become completely involved in their gift because they give of themselves as well as their money. They don't want to control how their gift is used, unless they are in the flesh, and that usually keeps the gift from being effective.

Givers love to show hospitality because they see it as another opportunity to give. They want to be a blessing to other people, whether it is materially, spiritually, or emotionally. They just say to the Lord, "I'm available for you to bless whoever You want, however You want, through me." Aren't they neat people? I want to be more like them.

Matthew reminds us to depend upon the Lord to meet our needs. Matthew 6:31 and 33 says, "Do not worry, saying 'What shall we eat?' or 'What shall we drink?' or 'What shall we wear?'...But seek first the kingdom of God and His righteousness, and all these things shall be added to you." In other words, if we put God first, He will meet our needs; He will take care of us. Matthew trusted God explicitly and wanted others to see that it really does work. Givers are always

The Gift of Giving

trying to push others toward a life of faith by trusting God to meet needs and sharing His blessings.

▶ **The giver is thrilled to discover that a gift is an answer to prayer and can be used as a blessing to others.**

Rate yourself:	Never	Seldom	Sometimes	Usually	Mostly	Always
	0	1	2	3	4	5

The giver gives the best because giving is seen as an investment of self. Givers primarily want to express love, and in the process, they give away a part of themselves. They are generous, maybe even lavish. A grandparent with this gift will spoil her grandchildren. She will go out of her way to give them everything a child could possibly want because that is the way she expresses her love. It can be a quandary for a parent, especially if that grandparent is in the flesh and tries to manipulate their family. A contest can develop to see who can out-give the others. They don't see anything wrong with giving the very best to the people they love because it represents a gift of themselves.

Matthew records in great detail the costly gifts that were brought to Jesus at His birth. It is Matthew who tells us about the woman who anointed Jesus with the precious ointment; and Matthew adds in 26:13 that Jesus says, "Assuredly, I say to you, wherever this gospel is preached in the whole world, what this woman has done will also be told as a memorial to her." Even though the other disciples were there, it didn't mean as much to them as it did to Matthew because giving was Matthew's special gift.

▶ **The giver gives the best because giving is seen as an investment of self.**

Rate yourself:	Never	Seldom	Sometimes	Usually	Mostly	Always
	0	1	2	3	4	5

Gifted for Life's Journey

Day Three

The giver practices personal thriftiness as a result of his contentment with the necessities of life. A person with this gift doesn't focus on getting luxuries for himself. He is frugal and doesn't waste money, especially on himself. He may wear the same clothes again and again and is content to use his possessions until they wear out. He will always shop for the best bargains. This is the person in front of you in the grocery store check-out line with a huge wad of coupons. She probably has more than enough money to pay for everything in her cart, but she will go through every one of those coupons because she doesn't want to waste a single penny.

Givers are fastidious in keeping records and believe everything must be accounted for, but they don't clutter up their lives with a lot of stuff. They are not usually pack rats. If they have something that someone else needs, they will give it to that person. They usually don't have yard sales because they would rather give things away than sell them.

Occasionally a young person will tell me that he is praying for God to make him a successful businessperson so that someday he will be able to give lots of money to the Lord. That is not the way it works. First, you give your heart to God; and then, if He wants you to be successful, He will take care of that. You must obey God, and do not tell Him how He should work in your life.

A giver would never presume upon God in that way. He is not interested in accumulating wealth. He is content with the basic necessities of life. He wants, more than anything else, to focus on God's will for his life. As long as you do that, He will make the resources available to you.

▶ **The giver practices personal thriftiness as a result of his contentment with the necessities of life.**

Rate yourself:

Never	Seldom	Sometimes	Usually	Mostly	Always
0	1	2	3	4	5

The giver demonstrates wisdom in investments and has success in handling business and financial matters. Whatever a giver touches seems to be blessed. They possess a natural business ability. These are the people who opened lemonade stands, when they were children, and made a huge profit. They were the kids in the neighborhood who were involved in entrepreneurial undertakings, like mowing yards or baby-sitting. They learned to save money at an early age.

They are not gullible or easily fooled. I believe God gives them that characteristic to protect them from those who would take advantage of them. You won't get something out of a giver by begging for it. They want to know that

78

The Gift of Giving

there is a specific need and that God can use them to meet that need. Givers have remarkable discernment coupled with wisdom.

► **The giver demonstrates wisdom in investments and has success in handling business and financial matters.**

Rate yourself:	Never	Seldom	Sometimes	Usually	Mostly	Always
	0	1	2	3	4	5

The giver spots financial needs that others miss. This is a characteristic that a giver has in common with a server. A server can see a need in someone's life, and will try to meet that need. A giver sees a financial need that he can meet, usually anonymously, and his response is to become personally involved. If someone is ill or in the hospital, the givers and the servers will be the first ones to take a meal to their family. Givers are always searching for a need to meet.

Givers are not shy about inquiring about a person's financial needs, but they do practice the art of discretion. They will not come up to you in public and ask if you have a need. Rather, they will call you on the phone or catch you when you're alone. Sometimes, they even investigate the need by asking others who might be aware of your situation. They don't want to hurt your feeling or make you feel obligated to repay them but they do feel a genuine burden for you and will go out of their way to meet your need.

► **The giver spots financial needs that others miss.**

Rate yourself:	Never	Seldom	Sometimes	Usually	Mostly	Always
	0	1	2	3	4	5

Day Four

The giver desires to use giving as a means to encourage others to give and to operate in the area of their giftedness. Givers believe strongly in giving to their local church. When controlled by the Holy Spirit, this person would never refuse to give his offering because he was disgruntled. He would never dream of using his propensity for giving to obtain a favor or to bend a decision in his direction. He sees giving as a sacred duty, not as a means of personal gain.

The famous businessman R. G. LeTourneau gave 90% of his earnings to the Lord's work and lived on the remaining 10%. I believe he was one of the best modern examples of one who had the gift of giving.

Gifted for Life's Journey

Matthew is the only gospel that records Christ's condemnation of the man who was forgiven much, but refused to forgive little. Those who have this particular gift desire, more than anything else, God's will to be done. They want to be a conduit for blessings to others and can't imagine shutting that off by putting strings on their giving.

I like being around givers because they challenge me to be faithful with my own gifts. They also challenge me to be faithful in those areas where I am weakest because they are so motivated by faith to follow God's direction.

▶ **The giver desires to use giving to encourage others to give and to operate in the area of their giftedness.**

Rate yourself:	Never	Seldom	Sometimes	Usually	Mostly	Always
	0	1	2	3	4	5

The Giver discerns with accuracy the spiritual condition of a person or situation based on his handling of finances. A giver has a remarkable capacity to discern a person's spiritual state based on how he handles his money. They understand the biblical principle found in Luke 16:10-11: that "He who is faithful in what is least is faithful also in much; and he who is unjust in what is least is unjust also in much." Their philosophy is, "Why should anybody be trusted with the greatest treasure of all, spiritual truth, if they can't handle the mundane material things of the world?" They are such good stewards of their own financial resources that they expect everyone else to be also.

It was Matthew who exposed the spiritual condition of others based on their handling of finances. He recorded that Judas betrayed Jesus for thirty pieces of silver. And Matthew tells us that when Judas returned the money, the religious leaders bought a field in which to bury strangers. He also tells us that the soldiers who guarded the tomb were paid by the high priest to lie and say that the disciples had stolen the body of Jesus.

Givers are naturally evangelistic. They love to tell others about Jesus because they know that the greatest gift of all is the gift of eternal life.

▶**The giver discerns with accuracy the spiritual condition of a person or situation based on his handling of finances.**

Rate yourself:	Never	Seldom	Sometimes	Usually	Mostly	Always
	0	1	2	3	4	5

The Gift of Giving

Your Score on the Gift of Giving

Take a few moments now to look back and copy your scores for this week. Add up your total points for the gift of giving at the bottom of the page.

_____ The giver is generous with money, possessions, time, energy, and love.

_____ The giver derives pleasure from giving without recognition.

_____ The giver believes God is the source and the motivation of giving.

_____ The giver is thrilled to discover that a gift is an answer to prayer and can be used as a blessing to others.

_____ The giver gives the best because giving is seen as an investment of self.

_____ The giver practices personal thriftiness as a result of his contentment with the necessities of life.

_____ The giver demonstrates wisdom in investments and has success in handling business and financial matters.

_____ The giver spots financial needs that others miss.

_____ The giver desires to use giving to encourage others to give and to operate in the area of their giftedness.

_____ The giver discerns with accuracy the spiritual condition of a person or situation based on his handling of finances.

_____ **Total Points**

Gifted for Life's Journey

Day Five

The Problems of the Gift of Giving

A giver who is in the flesh will be prone to exercise control through his money. If your child has this gift, the most important thing you can teach him is, that when he gives, he must do it with no strings attached.

A giver can lose his balance in regard to his family life and friends, if he loses his sensitivity to the Spirit of God. Givers tend to go two ways. They can either give so many things to their family that they lose their perspective in regard to material things, or they can become so involved in meeting the needs of others that they neglect the basic needs of their own family. Their own children may harbor bitterness and resentment because they see their parent meeting other people's needs, but not taking care of them. As a result, those closest to them are damaged spiritually.

The toughest struggle that a giver will face is to maintain balance in his life. In order to do this, he must remain sensitive to the Spirit of God through a daily quiet time. If he neglects his quiet time, it will begin to show; not only in his own walk with God, but also in the lives of those around him. He will also lose his ability to keep material things in their proper perspective and will use them to control others.

A giver operating in the flesh can be a terror when he is in control of the finances of a small church. He can shut everything down because he will bring his personal sin—that of using his giving to control others—into the confines of the church.

The Practice of the Gift of Giving

A Giver in the Spirit

When he is operating in the Spirit, this person can be described by seven words.

Thriftiness
A giver will be very frugal in his personal life.

The Gift of Giving

Resourcefulness

I love to watch a giver when she is told that something can't be accomplished with the resources that are available. She will take those resources and make them work. A giver who is operating in the Spirit is extremely resourceful.

Punctuality

A giver who is operating in the Spirit will always be punctual in order to make use of every minute. A giver who is married to a procrastinator will require the intervention of God to make that relationship work.

Tolerance

A giver is flexible where many others are not because he does not look at any situation as being the end result. He believes he can help change that situation. A giver will not be tolerant to the point of compromise, and a giver who is operating in the Spirit will retain strong morals.

Caution

A giver will not rush in to try to meet a particular need. Instead, he will be very cautious. He will first gather the facts to determine the need and how best to meet it.

Gratitude

A giver doesn't see himself as being special, but rather as a channel that God happens to be using. He is very grateful that God chooses to use him.

Contentment

Givers experience contented joy because they are using their gift and feel fulfilled in doing so.

A Giver in the Flesh

In contrast, there are seven words that describe this gift when it is misused.

Extravagance

A giver operating in the flesh will spend money extravagantly and foolishly. He loves to watch home shopping shows on TV or shop on the internet and will order anything, whether he needs it or not.

Wasteful

When the attitude of a giver is "easy come, easy go," he is living in the flesh.

Tardiness

They let opportunities slip right through their fingers. A giver operating in the Spirit views every situation as a golden opportunity to meet a need. When he is operating in the flesh, however, he loses the ability to see an opportunity to give and just lets it pass.

Prejudice

They will cater to certain people and ignore others. A giver in the flesh is arrogant, boastful, and proud. He will gravitate toward his own little group, and he usually has specific criteria for who gets into that group and who doesn't. As wonderful as they are in the Spirit, they are just as mean in the flesh.

Rashness

They make decisions without any forethought, doing whatever they feel like doing at that moment in time. This can be extremely costly and dangerous when they are operating in the flesh.

Ungratefulness

They aren't thankful because their focus is on their possessions and not on the Lord.

Frustrated covetousness

They aren't fulfilled in their giving because they can only think about getting what they want rather than giving to others. The giver has a tremendous capacity to be used by God. But in order to do this, he must first surrender control of himself to the Holy Spirit. Then he can be a channel for God's love to flow through him to others.

The Gift of Giving

Matthew's Example

The disciple Matthew is the best biblical example of this gift. His profession as a tax collector tells us something about his natural inclination. The book of Matthew has more advice on the wise use of money than any other gospel.

Matthew had wealth, but that didn't keep him from following Jesus. Luke 5:28 says of Matthew, "So he left all, rose up, and followed Him." Matthew wasn't so tied to his wealth that it kept him from doing God's will.

Matthew 6:20-21 says, "…but lay up for yourselves treasures in heaven, where neither moth nor rust destroys and where thieves do not break in and steal. For where your treasure is, there your heart will be also." Matthew tells us how we should handle our resources. We should not rely on earthly treasures or possessions, but rather store up treasures in heaven in the form of obedience to God.

Dealing With a Giver as a Child

A child with the gift of giving can be a tremendous blessing to a family, but is also a great challenge. The child's tendency, from the earliest age, will be to give everything away because of their immaturity in discerning when to give. Parents will be tempted to pressure these children to be less generous and often wound them with their lectures. Many of these children grow up frustrated by their parents' inability to understand this gift.

It is imperative that parents help children achieve balance in the exercise of this gift. One effective way to achieve this balance is by establishing three jars in which your child can deposit the weekly allowance you give them. Mark one jar *Jesus,* one jar *spend*, and one jar *save.* Give your child the freedom to use the money in her *spend* jar any way she chooses, within reason. Those children with the gift of giving will probably give it to others. Don't reprimand your child when she gives away a precious item or toy. Instead, teach your child discernment as to when one's possessions should be given away.

The greatest giver of all is God the Father. The Bible tells us in John 3:16, "For God so loved the world that He gave His only begotten Son, that whoever believes in Him should not perish but have everlasting life." God wants to give you the greatest gifts of all: eternal life, total fulfillment, abundant satisfaction, and a purpose that will last for all eternity. These gifts can only be found by believing in His Son, Jesus Christ, but they are free and can be yours if you will only ask Him.

Week Seven

The Gift of Administration

...he who leads, with diligence; Romans 12:8

Day One

The scripture refers to the administrator as he who leads. The Greek word for leader, as found in Romans 12:8, is *proistem,* which means the one who stands out front. We could call him an organizer or a born leader. This gift, along with the gift of prophesy, is one of the most misunderstood because people will mistake the administrator's drive to achieve a leadership role as egotism and will resent his attempts to control others around him.

The Personality of the Administrator

An administrator visualizes the end result and the broad perspective of any major undertaking. Administrators thrive on long-range goals. A server will be frustrated if you give him a project that lasts more than two weeks. But if you want to make an administrator happy, give him a two-year project with intermediate goals along the way. Administrators love to attend time management seminars to learn how to manage their time and handle those long-range projects. Their greatest fulfillment is in working toward and anticipating the end result as the intermediate goals are accomplished one by one.

An administrator stays focused on the big picture. These people are usually great leaders and people of vision. They will challenge an organization or a group to stretch itself and to achieve enormous results. When they are operating in the Spirit, they keep a tremendous sense of direction because they can visualize the accomplishment of a goal. Any church or group must have someone with this gift in order to function properly.

Administrators are able to ignore distracting details and to remain focused in order to keep everyone moving toward the end result. They have the capacity to

The Gift of Administration

see far beyond most people and to say, "This is where we should go, and here are the goals that we must accomplish in order to get there." They are motivated to look ahead, to visualize the end result, and to grasp the broad perspective.

▶ **An administrator visualizes the end result and the broad perspective of any major undertaking.**

Rate yourself:	Never	Seldom	Sometimes	Usually	Mostly	Always
	0	1	2	3	4	5

An administrator accepts responsibility for a project and quickly moves to organize that project. Administrators are natural and capable leaders. They love to organize anything. Give them a kitchen cabinet or an office, and they will organize it. My wife has this gift, and everything in every drawer or closet in our home is in order.

Administrators also love to lead. They have the ability to organize people, and they will assume leadership of a group when no one else is in charge. If a church committee isn't functioning properly or accomplishing anything, put an administrator in the group. He will step up and get them moving. They are motivated by a desire to lead others.

Because of their natural leadership abilities, administrators must be careful not to step on toes or hurt others' feelings. Sometimes, people who do not have the gift of administrator resent being bossed about by those who do. They may voice their resentment by saying something like, "Who put you in charge?" The administrator must guard against such conflict by leading gracefully. By asking the other members of the group for their advice and opinions, the administrator can incorporate them into his leadership strategy.

Nehemiah 2:7-8 illustrates the way an administrator thinks. In presenting his plan to rebuild the walls of Jerusalem to the king, Nehemiah gave an organized report saying, "... 'If it pleases the king, let letters be given to me for the governors of the region beyond the River, and a letter to Asaph the keeper of the king's forest, that he must give me timber to make beams for the gates of the citadel which pertains to the temple, for the city wall, and for the house that I will occupy.' And the king granted them to me according to the good hand of my God upon me."

In other words, Nehemiah went to the king and said, "Here is a list of things we need to do, and these are the resources I need to accomplish them." That is the way an administrator operates.

Gifted for Life's Journey

▶**An administrator accepts responsibility for a project and quickly moves to organize that project.**

Rate yourself:	Never	Seldom	Sometimes	Usually	Mostly	Always
	0	1	2	3	4	5

Day Two

An administrator possesses a remarkable ability to subdivide long-range goals into smaller tasks. How do you eat an elephant? One bite at a time. It doesn't matter to an administrator how big a project is. They are not discouraged by the size of the task because they will break it down into bite-sized chunks. Administrators organize their lives by lists and write everything down so that they will not forget their goals.

Nehemiah accomplished the huge task of rebuilding the walls around Jerusalem by dividing the wall into small sections and assigning each family to work on a portion of the wall. God used Nehemiah's natural inclination to lead the people in rebuilding the wall.

▶**An administrator possesses a remarkable ability to subdivide long-range goals into smaller tasks.**

Rate yourself:	Never	Seldom	Sometimes	Usually	Mostly	Always
	0	1	2	3	4	5

An administrator prefers to operate by the principle of authority in the acceptance and delegation of responsibility, whether they are in charge or not. They want to know their boundaries. They want to know if they are outside of the guidelines and what authority they have. If they are not the leader, they prefer to be left alone to function as their own boss in their own area. If an administrator is working for you, then you can tell him what needs to be done and turn him loose. He will have the capacity to organize the project, break it down into smaller tasks, and carry through until it is accomplished.

The Gift of Administration

Unlike many people, an administrator understands one of the most important leadership skills—how to delegate tasks. If a person doesn't learn to delegate, he will never be very effective. But administrators run the risk of delegating everything and becoming lazy or losing touch with the organization. An administrator who is functioning in the Spirit knows how to decide which tasks should be delegated and which should not be.

Nehemiah knew which tasks to delegate and which not to delegate. We see in Nehemiah 4 that he delegated the manual labor for the building of the wall, but he personally assumed the role of the sergeant-at-arms in order to insure that the children of Israel were protected as they built the wall.

▶**An administrator prefers to operate by the principle of authority in the acceptance and delegation of responsibility.**

Rate yourself:	Never	Seldom	Sometimes	Usually	Mostly	Always
	0	1	2	3	4	5

Day Three

An administrator utilizes the appropriate resources and people to accomplish goals. Administrators set goals, establish intermediate tasks to reach the goals, and then assess the available resources. That is a great way to solve any problem. They can plan the steps necessary to accomplish a task and understand how to use available resources. They then begin delegating to others.

Administrators, when operating in the Spirit, are usually very secure people and have no problem sharing recognition with others. All an administrator really cares about is getting the job done.

It is great to have someone with the gift of administration in a staff meeting. Others will be explaining why something can't be done, or someone will object and say, "We've never done it that way before." The administrator, meanwhile, will have already begun planning to see that the job gets done. They have the capacity to carry a job through to completion.

Many churches are hindered by people who just love to tell you the reasons why you *can't* do something. I believe God is so great and so wonderful that, if He calls us to do something, He can finish it. We don't have to worry about our human limitations. An administrator can envision plans coming to fruition. I believe administrators are placed in the church by God to show us what we can do when we depend on God's resources.

Nehemiah, for example, came to Jerusalem with all the resources necessary to rebuild the wall. He brought letters from the king for the timber and rebuilt the wall within about fifty days. He built that wall while everyone else was wringing their hands and saying it couldn't be done. Nehemiah got the job done because he was operating under the leadership of the Holy Spirit.

▶ **An administrator utilizes the appropriate resources and people to accomplish goals.**

Rate yourself:	Never	Seldom	Sometimes	Usually	Mostly	Always
	0	1	2	3	4	5

An administrator accepts criticism from others as a necessary part of reaching the ultimate goal. If you are ever placed in a leadership position, rest assured you will be criticized. I have seen pastors and business people fail more often because of this than for any other reason. If you don't do anything, someone will criticize you; but if you do something, they will still criticize you because they don't like the *way* you do it.

Criticism doesn't bother an administrator because he has skin as tough as a rhinoceros' hide. An administrator will listen to you, look at the situation to see if your advice applies, then make adjustments as necessary. You may come back later and apologize for being overly critical, and he will look at you with a blank stare. He has forgotten about it because it didn't bother him.

Those who have the gifts of service or mercy will lie awake at night worrying about critical comments. An administrator knows he will be criticized because he is a mover and a shaker. He is willing to take whatever criticism is necessary to reach the ultimate goal.

Churches everywhere are dying because their leaders fold under criticism. Pastors and leaders in the church need to be very aware that, whenever God is doing something in a tremendous way, Satan will use criticism to upset people. We've all had our feelings hurt because of criticism; that will continue to happen as long as we are out front doing God's will. An administrator understands that, if he is on the cutting edge, he will be cut every now and then. Someone will always come along to find fault. But an administrator also thinks, "That makes no difference, as long as I know I am following God's leadership."

Even Jesus' feelings could be hurt. Remember the time he wept over Jerusalem? Pray for anyone you know who is an administrator because, I promise you, he is taking more than his fair share of criticism. Whether he is exercising leadership in his home, his business, or in his church, he is moving people out of their comfort zones to make sure that things are being accomplished.

The Gift of Administration

An administrator is concerned about what works and what doesn't. If an accepted practice is not in accordance with God's will, then the administrator's approach is to change that practice until it is in the center of God's will, even if he is criticized by others.

Nehemiah encountered tremendous criticism. There were two particular critics, Tobiah and Sanballat, who did everything they could to discourage Nehemiah, but he kept pressing on to accomplish what needed to be done.

▶ **An administrator accepts criticism from others as a necessary part of reaching the ultimate goal.**

Rate yourself:	Never	Seldom	Sometimes	Usually	Mostly	Always
	0	1	2	3	4	5

An administrator enjoys motivating and working with people. They love to be with groups of people as long as they can lead those people. Don't ask them to follow blindly because they are born shepherds who are motivated to lead. They look for ways to interact more effectively with people. Administrators are the ones who like to use things like colored charts and PowerPoint to enhance their presentation.

They don't need to receive credit for everything they do. In fact, they love to share the spotlight with others. If you have recognized an administrator for the fine job he has done on a project, he'll say, "It couldn't have happened without this group of people around me." That is not false humility; the administrator simply sees himself as one who can facilitate others into accomplishing the tasks that need to be done.

Nehemiah tells us that, after the wall was rebuilt, he found a register of the genealogy of Israel. He spoke to the people about the heritage they enjoyed as believers in God and reminded them that the work of rebuilding the wall had depended on the work that had been done earlier. It was Nehemiah's way of saying, "This is not just our success. It is shared with all those who came before us."

▶ **An administrator enjoys motivating and working with people.**

Rate yourself:	Never	Seldom	Sometimes	Usually	Mostly	Always
	0	1	2	3	4	5

Gifted for Life's Journey

Day Four

An administrator displays loyalty and expects loyalty when interacting with others. Nothing grieves an administrator like disloyalty because he looks at the big picture. When he sees disloyalty in one part of the project, he sees the effect that it has on the complete institution or the ultimate goal. He is gratified to see a goal accomplished and is disturbed when he sees something in the works that could endanger that goal. An administrator will become extremely upset when the pieces do not fit together because someone allowed his ego to get in the way. An administrator dislikes disloyalty in those who are supposed to be following him because this impedes an orderly progression toward a goal.

Administrators easily give loyalty to those who are leading them; they understand how the principle of authority operates. They know they can't lead someone else until they are aligned with their own leader.

Nehemiah required the people to enter into an oath of loyalty to God after the wall was rebuilt. In Nehemiah 10:29, he told them that they were to commit "...to observe and do all the commandments of the Lord our Lord, and His ordinances and His statutes."

▶**An administrator displays loyalty and expects loyalty in interaction with others.**

Rate yourself:	**Never**	**Seldom**	**Sometimes**	**Usually**	**Mostly**	**Always**
	0	**1**	**2**	**3**	**4**	**5**

An administrator approaches each task with great enthusiasm, until the major goal is accomplished, and then prefers to move quickly to a new challenge. Enthusiasm exudes from an administrator. He becomes excited and involved in what he does. Romans 12:8 describes this gift as, "he who leads, with diligence." The Greek word *spoude* means intense eagerness and effort.

God has created the administrator to throw all his energy into a project and to give himself wholeheartedly to a task. Many times the zeal of the administrator will overwhelm and intimidate other people. Once the goal is met, the administrator will be equally zealous about a new project because he is satisfied with the accomplishment of the goal and ready to move on to the next.

He doesn't like to just keep the routine going. Don't give an administrator a position and say, "Just maintain the status quo." He wants the challenge of

The Gift of Administration

plowing new ground or moving into unexplored territory. He wants to be on the cutting edge, charting the course for the future.

They certainly don't like delays that keep them from accomplishing their goals. Don't tie them down with red tape. The attitude of an administrator is, "I have a job to do; I want to do it as well and as quickly as possible."

Some of Nehemiah's detractors wanted him to stop working in order to meet with them. I love his response in Nehemiah 6:3, "So I sent messengers to them, saying, 'I am doing a great work, so that I cannot come down'."

▶ **An administrator approaches each task with great enthusiasm until the major goal is accomplished and then prefers to move quickly to a new challenge.**

Rate yourself:	Never	Seldom	Sometimes	Usually	Mostly	Always
	0	1	2	3	4	5

An administrator derives great fulfillment from seeing a goal accomplished. He becomes bored with routine things such as assembly line work and repetitive responsibilities. You can give a server a repetitive task, and he will be fulfilled because he is happy just to do something. A smart administrator recruits servers to work for him because, in that way, they will both be fulfilled.

A homemaker who is an administrator will hate the routine of cleaning house, and an administrator husband will dislike mowing the lawn. If they can't afford to hire someone else to do it for them, you will see them wearing headphones or doing something else simultaneously to help dispel the boredom of the task. Their joy is in seeing intermediate tasks fall together like pieces in a puzzle until the big picture comes into focus. They don't need praise or expressions of appreciation. It is enough for them to see the goal accomplished. Every organization needs someone who enjoys seeing things come together.

Nehemiah expressed his joy in the completion of the wall by leading the people in a great celebration. Nehemiah 8:10 says, "...the joy of the Lord is your strength."

▶ **An administrator derives great fulfillment from seeing a goal accomplished.**

Rate yourself:	Never	Seldom	Sometimes	Usually	Mostly	Always
	0	1	2	3	4	5

Gifted for Life's Journey

Your Score on the Gift of Administration

Take a few moments now to look back and copy your scores for this week on the characteristics of the gift of administration. Write down your total points at the bottom of the page.

_____ An administrator visualizes the end result and the broad perspective of any major undertaking.

_____ An administrator accepts responsibility for a project and quickly moves to organize that project.

_____ An administrator possesses a remarkable ability to subdivide long-range goals into smaller tasks.

_____ An administrator prefers to operate by the principle of authority in the acceptance and delegation of responsibility.

_____ An administrator utilizes the appropriate resources and people to accomplish goals.

_____ An administrator accepts criticism from others as a necessary part of reaching the ultimate goal.

_____ An administrator enjoys motivating and working with people.

_____ An administrator displays loyalty and expects loyalty in interaction with others.

_____ An administrator approaches each task with great enthusiasm until the major goal is accomplished and then prefers to move quickly to a new challenge.

_____ An administrator derives great fulfillment from seeing a goal accomplished.

_____ Total Points

The Gift of Administration

Day Five

The Problems of the Gift of Administration

An administrator can grow hardened to criticism, and then you can't get through to him. He decides that no one else knows what they are talking about, and it is very hard to get his attention. An administrator must maintain a close walk with God, or he will lose his sensitivity to the Holy Spirit; otherwise, projects will become more important than people. They will be driven to merely accomplish goals and will begin to view people as pawns.

A good leader delegates, but also stays in touch with his people. An administrator who is not functioning according to the leading of the Holy Spirit will delegate everything, lose interest, and become lazy. An administrator in the flesh can also go to the opposite extreme. He can become so involved in the process that he will overload those he is supposed to be leading. Because administrators are so focused on the big picture and so driven to accomplish goals, they can be tempted to use any means to accomplish the goal.

It is dangerous to follow an insecure leader because he will try to make himself look good. In order to show himself in a better light, he may try to make the people around him look bad. Many times, what appears to be arrogance, pride, and egotism, is really insecurity and the leader's attempt to garner respect from those people around him.

Some churches have worthy goals and would like to see great things happen for Jesus Christ, but they forget that *how* you achieve those goals is just as important as the actual accomplishment of those goals. An administrator who has lost sight of his responsibility before God will adopt the idea that the end justifies the means. He may badger people instead of praising them, and he doesn't give them the information necessary to see the overall picture.

An administrator can even neglect his family because he is so wrapped up in the pursuit of a particular goal. He needs to be careful that projects don't become more important than his own family. He can become impatient with others, whom he believes are not moving swiftly enough. Sometimes God will purposely put a procrastinator with an administrator to teach that person patience and trust in God. An administrator may jump ahead and provide premature leadership that is unnecessary.

Gifted for Life's Journey

The Practice of the Gift of Administration

An Administrator in the Spirit

There are seven ways to tell if an administrator is operating in the Spirit.

Order

He will be organized in his thinking. He will properly use the resources available to him.

Initiative

He is a self-starter. He sees a goal and begins moving toward it on his own.

Responsibility

He is willing to accept responsibility and to use the authority he has been given.

Humility

If an administrator functions with a submissive, humble spirit, then he can maintain his loyalty and commitment to Christ and will be motivated by love. He won't be intimidating, domineering, or dictatorial. He can paint the big picture and see its value and its cost; he can motivate others to get in on the blessing. An administrator constantly fights the battle to remain humble. He must remember that God has called us to humble ourselves at His feet. If you happen to be bent in this direction, you must give specific attention to maintaining a humble walk.

Determination

If you ask an administrator to make a decision, you will get one. If he is operating in the Spirit, he can make decisions at times when everyone else is wavering. He will be able to step in, even when his leadership is unpopular, and he is willing to pay a price to accomplish the goal. He can make the commitment, close the door on further discussion, and make adjustments as needed. He can operate on the basis of determination alone.

Loyalty

An administrator is loyal to those with whom he works and he, in turn, expects loyalty from others.

Joy

It is wonderful to be around a joyful administrator because he is so fulfilled.

An Administrator in the Flesh

As wonderful as it is to be around a spiritual administrator, it is dreadful to be around an administrator in the flesh. There are seven words to describe them.

Disorganization

When an administrator is in the flesh, he allows things to get into disarray. This heightens his level of frustration because he doesn't function well in a disorderly environment.

Laziness

An administrator in the flesh lets himself and his environment go. He neglects his responsibilities and becomes apathetic.

Irresponsibility

The word of an administrator means nothing when he is operating in the flesh, and you can't trust him.

Egotism

They become dictatorial and dogmatic, and they demand to have their way. They lead, not by love, but rather, by intimidation. The first thing that goes when an administrator gets in the flesh is his humility because pride moves in, arrogance takes over, and you can't move him. He has made up his mind.

Indecisiveness

When an administrator is functioning in the flesh, you'll hear him say things like, "I think so, but I'm not sure." He will see obstacles everywhere. Instead of moving on with determination, he will become fearful. He gets sidetracked and loses his confidence.

Unfaithfulness

They will drop out of church and begin to go in other directions. They will no longer be faithful to their commitments and will lose focus on their goals.

Frustration

They will live an unfulfilled life.

Nehemiah's Example

The most outstanding biblical person with the gift of the administrator is Nehemiah. The entire book of Nehemiah is filled with examples of his effective leadership. He was working in the king's court when he heard that the walls of Jerusalem had been torn down. He had a vision to rebuild the walls in order to remove the reproach from his people. He then kept himself focused on the achievement of that goal until the walls were finished.

Nehemiah 2:5 records, "And I said to the king, 'If it pleases the king, and if your servant has found favor in your sight, I ask that you send me to Judah, to the city of my fathers' tombs, that I may rebuild it'." Nehemiah had the vision to accomplish his goal.

Dealing With an Administrator as a Child

Dealing with a child who has the gift of administration can be one of the greatest challenges a parent faces. Children with this gift will often tend to dominate their siblings and will, in fact, be very bossy. If the parent has the gift of service or mercy, there may even be a tendency for the child to attempt to lead the parent. If your child has the gift of administration, begin giving them responsibilities at an early age with ever increasing importance. Start by giving

The Gift of Administration

them the task of keeping their room picked up. Assign each toy and item in their room a specific place, and reward your child with an allowance when he puts everything back in its place.

Be careful not to let your administrator child take over the family. As your child approaches the teen years, set appropriate boundaries that she can clearly understand. If she violates those boundaries, be swift to implement the prescribed corrections for that behavior; your administrator will understand. It is imperative that you give your child consistent reinforcement and praise when she honors your expectations. Also, consistently impress upon your child how very valuable she is to you, your family, and to God. This will keep her from struggling with the insecurity that plagues so many with the gift of administration.

Just as Nehemiah led God's people to do what many thought to be impossible, so the administrator, led and empowered by God, can do more than most people to advance the kingdom. Remember, however, that an administrator's capacity to lead is in direct proportion to the level of his willingness to follow God's direction in his own life. An administrator, completely surrendered to the will of God, will inspire others to reach for all that God wants to do in their own situation.

Week Eight

The Gift of Mercy

… he who shows mercy, with cheerfulness. *Romans 12:8*

Day One

The word *cheerful* in Romans 12:8 is the same word from which we get our word *hilarity*. When a mercy-giver is operating in the power of the Spirit, he will have an exceeding joy, but when he is not in the Spirit, he will be extremely frustrated.

The motivational gifts can be divided into two categories: the speaking gifts and the serving gifts. The speaking gifts include prophecy, teaching, exhortation, and administration. These must communicate verbally in some way to function. The prophet discerns between what is and is not God's will. The administrator outlines the steps that need to be taken. The exhorter encourages people to move on to achieve their potential. The teacher communicates truth he has discovered.

The serving gifts include service, giving, and mercy. These people must work to meet a need. Mercy relates best with mercy and least with the prophet. If a prophet and a mercy-giver allow themselves to be controlled by the flesh, you can have a battle on your hands. The mercy-giver will retreat inside when he is hurt, and the prophet will find and confront the source of the problem. It is unusual for two people with the same gift to marry each other, but if two mercy-givers do marry, they will usually have a long and happy marriage. They will be committed to meeting each other's needs and taking care of each other.

The Personality of the Mercy-giver

A mercy-giver possesses a tremendous capacity to love and to discern genuine love when exhibited by others. They hurt on a deep level for other people and will enter into others' sorrow and pain. The more opportunities they have to show love, the more fulfilled they feel. They can see the difference between

The Gift of Mercy

genuine and phony love much easier than those without this gift. They can quickly spot hypocrisy or insincerity in others and will draw away from them. They like to look for the good in people, and it grieves their spirit to hear anything negative. They have the capacity to sense the spiritual and emotional condition of another. They are able to walk into a room and tell whether people are happy or sad. They are alert to body language as well as spoken words.

They are experts at discerning where people are spiritually. I love to have a mercy-giver present when I interview someone because I can see in black and white, but he can discern nuances in the other person's character.

▶ **A mercy-giver possesses a tremendous capacity to love and to discern genuine love when exhibited by others.**

Rate yourself:	Never	Seldom	Sometimes	Usually	Mostly	Always
	0	1	2	3	4	5

A mercy-giver focuses on the spiritual and emotional distress of others rather than his own physical distress. They are not worried about physical needs, but rather about spiritual pain and meeting the needs of people who hurt. Sometimes it is very difficult for a mercy-giver to help someone because he is so caring, and he hurts intensely with them.

A mercy-giver feels an intense need to bring mercy to bear in another person's life, but sometimes forgets that mercy may keep the other person from realizing the benefits of suffering. Those with the gift of mercy must be careful not to step in and try to remove the hurt that God intends for the person to experience.

For example, God may be taking somebody through a corrective situation so that he will turn away from a particular sin. Many times a mercy-giver will not understand why the suffering is occurring and will try to take away the suffering. Because he is so anxious to bring joy and happiness to people, he doesn't want others to feel sad or negative.

In the apostle John's letters, he used the words *that your joy may be full.* That is why Romans 12:8 says that the one who shows mercy should do so with hilarity or joy.

▶ **A mercy-giver focuses on the spiritual and emotional distress of others rather than his own physical distress.**

Rate yourself:	Never	Seldom	Sometimes	Usually	Mostly	Always
	0	1	2	3	4	5

Gifted for Life's Journey

Day Two

A mercy-giver attracts people who are hurting. If a mercy-giver senses that someone in the room has a problem, the two will come together like a bee to honey. The mercy-giver exudes compassion, so he can get someone to talk about his problem, even if the person doesn't realize he has a problem. He has the capacity to dig deep into a person's life and cause that person to share his most personal experiences. The person who is gifted with mercy has a tremendous capacity to attract people who are hurting.

The mercy-giver is driven to alleviate the distress of others. He will look past his own physical needs directly into the hearts and lives of the people near him. He is compelled by compassion to meet their needs. A person with sympathy says, "I see that you are hurting, and I am sorry." A person with empathy says, "I see that you are hurting, and I am sorry. I will hurt with you." But a person who has compassion says, "I see that you are hurting, and I am sorry. I will hurt with you, and I will stay with you until the hurt is past." The person who has the gift of mercy just wants to shield you with compassion.

Mercy-givers grieve over broken relationships, and it breaks their heart to see people fighting or angry. They will say, "I'm wrong," even when they are not at fault, in order to make sure that others are at peace with them. They are deeply wounded by negative and critical statements, especially about other people. They will be grieved, but only on rare occasions will they have enough fortitude to confront you.

They will, however, carry deep wounds caused by comments that would just roll off the back of a prophet. I've had people make a digging or catty remark to me, and being a prophet, I think, "That's their problem, not mine. If they want to be bitter, then just let them be." It won't disturb my sleep at all. But I've had a mercy-giver overhear the critical remark and get so upset that he sends me a sweet card or flowers the next day because he is so wounded for me. They will be hurt and try to reach out when someone makes a negative or critical statement because they want to bring an end to pain.

Many times they will take on much more than they are capable of bearing, which makes them feel frustrated. They must realize they can't meet all those needs and still preserve their own identity.

▶ **A mercy-giver attracts people who are hurting.**

Rate yourself:	Never	Seldom	Sometimes	Usually	Mostly	Always
	0	1	2	3	4	5

The Gift of Mercy

A mercy-giver looks for opportunities to give preference to others. Mercy-givers are thoughtful and have a remarkable capacity to be kind to others. They are the ones who stop their cars in heavy traffic, causing wrecks behind them, to let someone else pull out. They are the first ones in a crowded room to get up and say, "Won't you please take my seat?" They remember anniversaries and birthdays, and always send the perfect card. They know exactly what to say and how to say it.

These are the husbands about whom other wives say, "Why can't my husband be like him?" They are very affectionate. Watch them in public with their wives, and you will hear them use endearments like, Sugar and Honey. These are also the wives who make candlelight dinners. They are the friends who put so much effort into a relationship. You may go for two or three months without contacting them, but they are writing you a card or calling you every week.

They want to stay in the background and never want credit for anything they do in the church. If you call a mercy-giver up to the podium to express your appreciation for him, you will hurt him because he doesn't want to be in the spotlight. They will go to extreme lengths to avoid causing pain to others. They are so careful about what they say because they don't want to say anything that will offend someone else.

If mercy people have a big problem, it is the need to be accepted by others. They are distressed when someone doesn't accept them, even if it is for the wrong reason. If they are rejected by a non-believer for taking a stand for their Christian values, they are deeply hurt. They think, "Why don't they love God like I do? Look how much He cares for us." They cannot understand why anyone would reject Jesus Christ.

They love to touch and hug you. They want to hold your hand when they talk. Physical closeness, more than anything else, recharges their battery. If you are married to a mercy-giver or have a child with this gift, they need lots of hugs and kisses.

If you are a prophet, you are going to have to bend over backwards and go against your own nature to fulfill the affectionate needs of the mercy-giver in your home. You may not like it, but it has to be done. They need to know that you care very deeply about them.

John was always close to Jesus, even within the inner circle. In the Scriptures John calls himself the disciple whom Jesus loved. This shows us that Jesus recognized that John had a need to be loved. I can imagine Jesus walking along with His arm around John, and John reaching out to shake Jesus' hand. It was John who rested his head on Jesus in the upper room. He needed that physical closeness and contact.

▶ **A mercy-giver looks for opportunities to give preference to others.**

Rate yourself:	**Never**	**Seldom**	**Sometimes**	**Usually**	**Mostly**	**Always**
	0	**1**	**2**	**3**	**4**	**5**

Gifted for Life's Journey

Day Three

A mercy-giver postpones decisions and conflicts except when eliminating great hurts. A mercy-giver doesn't know how to be firm. He will put his hands on his hips and act tough, but soon he will melt into a pile of mush. He avoids confrontation at all costs. He won't say what he really thinks, and he will often beat around the bush.

Conflict deeply grieves a mercy-giver. Divorce is one of the most overwhelming and damaging things a mercy-giver can ever face. It ravages his soul, no matter if he is going through it personally or if someone he loves goes through it. A child will blame himself for his parents' divorce and will carry that burden for the rest of his life, unless he can learn to deal with his guilt properly by asking for God's intervention.

Because they dislike conflict so much, mercy-givers will interject themselves into a fight and try to stop it. They have a hard time getting out of the way, and letting God use suffering in a person's life to teach him a valuable lesson. Unless they are very responsive to the leadership of the Holy Spirit, they can short circuit God's work in a person's life.

One of the most dangerous parenting situations I know is when a parent has the gift of mercy. She will not let her child learn the tough lessons of life, but will try to step in and shield the child. Her child may become very disobedient because she refuses to properly discipline him and cause that child any displeasure. She must be careful to maintain balance in her gift for the child's own good.

John was able to achieve that balance. One of the greatest spiritual lessons in Scripture is John's capacity for having the gift of mercy, yet being bold and confrontational when he needed to be. Acts 4:13 describes Peter and John: "Now when they saw the boldness of Peter and John, and perceived that they were uneducated men and untrained men, they marveled." I can understand Peter the prophet being outspoken, but where did John learn to be that bold?

It is interesting that Jesus brought both Peter the prophet and John the mercy-giver into his inner circle. Usually, the prophet is the least gifted in the area of mercy, and the mercy-giver is the least gifted in the area of prophecy. They needed each other to provide balance and to accomplish what God called them to do.

▶ **A mercy-giver postpones decisions and conflicts except when eliminating great hurts.**

Rate yourself:	Never	Seldom	Sometimes	Usually	Mostly	Always
	0	1	2	3	4	5

The Gift of Mercy

A mercy-giver needs deep friendships which exhibit mutual loyalty and commitment. If you have a mercy-giver for a friend, you have him for life. He will be loyal and committed, caring and concerned. He gives every fiber of his being to a relationship and expects commitment in return; otherwise he feels hurt and wonders why his friend doesn't feel as committed to the friendship. He will blame himself when relationships go wrong.

Mercy-givers are very trustworthy and expect others to be also. They expect the best from a person and are always looking on the bright side. They can be very gullible and will trust almost anybody. They are distressed when someone lets them down or betrays a friendship.

The only time a mercy-giver will become confrontational is when someone attacks a friend or family member that he loves. He will rise up in their defense. He won't be extremely bold in his confrontation, unless he has matured spiritually, but he will react with a degree of harshness if necessary.

You need to understand the personality of a mercy-giver to understand John's reaction when Jesus and the disciples were rejected. Luke 9:54 says, "And when His disciples James and John saw this, they said, 'Lord do You want us to command fire to come down from heaven and consume them, just as Elijah did?'" I am always amused when I read John's response. Because someone he loved had been rejected, he was ready to confront the offenders. It's as if he were saying, "Just give us the word, Lord, and we will smoke them!"

A prophet is just the opposite of a mercy-giver and often prefers to be alone. He can't understand why mercy-givers want family and friends around all the time, hugging and kissing each other. Mercy-givers need close personal friendships.

▶ **A mercy-giver needs deep friendships which exhibit mutual loyalty and commitment.**

Rate yourself:	Never	Seldom	Sometimes	Usually	Mostly	Always
	0	1	2	3	4	5

A mercy-giver enjoys a special unity with those who are sensitive to the needs and feelings of others. You won't see mercy-givers around a bunch of critics. If you have a sour attitude, he will still be your friend, but he will not go out of his way to spend time with you. They are particularly attracted to others who share their gift. Mercy-givers cluster together in coveys, hugging each other and meeting each others' emotional needs. Nothing excites them more than finding someone who is sad. They flock to that person and bolster him up. Then they all cry together and hug because they are so happy. They love to spend time with others who share the same concerns.

Gifted for Life's Journey

▶**A mercy-giver enjoys a special unity with those who are sensitive to the needs and feelings of others.**

Rate yourself:	Never	Seldom	Sometimes	Usually	Mostly	Always
	0	1	2	3	4	5

Day Four

A mercy-giver possesses an inner joy that can rejoice when others are blessed and weep when others are hurt. Mercy-givers are positive people. They enjoy showing love to others. Mercy-givers must be on constant guard against the tendency to give away even their virtue because of their intense need to be loved.

They identify with others. If you share good news with them, they are glad for you. If you share bad news, they will be sad with you. There are times when you don't need more advice or an evaluation, but just someone to listen. A mercy-giver will offer encouragement and a sympathetic shoulder to cry on

They will often pray about the problems and the sufferings of others. I can tell a great deal about a person's heart by listening to the way they focus on God in their prayers. Three of the gifts are especially drawn to prayer. The prophet is drawn to prayer because he wants to pray for God's will. The giver is drawn to pray for direction in how to give of himself. The mercy-giver is drawn to intercessory prayer for people.

John continually emphasized prayer. He alone records the prayer in John 17 that Jesus prayed on our behalf. He was especially sensitive to prayer because of his gift of mercy.

▶**A mercy-giver possesses an inner joy that can rejoice when others are blessed and weep when others are hurt.**

Rate yourself:	Never	Seldom	Sometimes	Usually	Mostly	Always
	0	1	2	3	4	5

The Gift of Mercy

A mercy-giver relies on emotion rather than logic to guide him. Until I learned this, I continued to have conflicts with mercy-givers. I would come into a meeting, and use my prophetic gift to outline all the logical reasons why something was God's will. My presentation would be precise and to the point, then some person with the gift of mercy would say, "But I just don't feel like we need to do this." I would think, "Feelings don't have anything to do with it! I've given you a logical explanation of why we ought to do this!"

A person with the gift of mercy doesn't want to deal with logic or point-by-point explanations. He doesn't need an analysis. He buys a car because of its color. It doesn't matter that it doesn't have an engine! He makes his decisions on the basis of emotion.

Don't misunderstand me; they are not dumb. Their heart is the channel that God uses to work through them. The prophet tends to be more intellectual, and the teacher is definitely intellectual, but the mercy-giver is very expressive with his emotions. They cry at the drop of a hat. They love to watch old tear-jerker movies and weep their hearts out over them. They are very tenderhearted.

Many times, people may make derogatory comments about the mercy-giver's tendency to cry and show his emotions. That can squelch the mercy-giver's spirit and cause him to suppress his emotions more and more.

Don't ask a mercy-giver to plan anything or arrive anywhere on time because he makes decisions on the spur of the moment. You may as well stop trying to rush him. They don't even know why clocks were made. They drive prophets and administrators crazy because meeting people's needs or holding someone's hand and sympathizing with that person is infinitely more important to them than meeting any deadline.

They readily allow themselves to be interrupted. It is rare for a mercy-giver to be able to complete a project because they find themselves pulled in various directions by needs that must be met. They allow themselves to be interrupted because their motivation is to infuse love into situations, and they let love take priority over everything else. They rely more on their emotions than schedules.

▶ **A mercy-giver relies on emotion rather than logic to guide him.**

Rate yourself:	Never	Seldom	Sometimes	Usually	Mostly	Always
	0	1	2	3	4	5

Gifted for Life's Journey

A mercy-giver takes a stand when the cause is right. There are times when a mercy-giver has no other choice but to take a stand because he sees a great wrong occurring. Usually, those who take the strongest stands against abortion are the mercy-givers because they empathize with the unborn child. They are compelled, by virtue of the suffering and pain they feel for that child, to take up the cause and make a stand on the issue.

I am convinced that many of the hippies and flower children in the 1960s had the gift of mercy. It could have been so great, if the church had known how to evangelize them. The last thing you want to do is ram truth down the throat of a person with the gift of mercy, and that is what the church tried to do. As a result, many of them turned their back on the church. If we had handled that correctly, I believe that this nation would have been in a state of spiritual awakening today. Instead, an entire generation of baby boomers ended up in a state of spiritual confusion. We mishandled this group of people and allowed a wonderful opportunity to slip through our fingers.

Others deserted Jesus and ran away when He was arrested. Peter cursed and swore he didn't even know Jesus. But John was standing there at the foot of the cross with Jesus' mother. I imagine he felt the nails as they were driven into Jesus' hands and feet as he watched with a broken heart, weeping for his Savior whom he loved. He was compelled to stand at the cross and identify himself with Jesus even though everyone else had deserted Him.

▶ **A mercy-giver takes a stand when the cause is right.**

Rate yourself:	Never	Seldom	Sometimes	Usually	Mostly	Always
	0	1	2	3	4	5

The Gift of Mercy

Rate Yourself on the Gift of Mercy

As we do each week, take a few moments now to look back and copy your scores for this week on the characteristics of the gift of mercy. Write down your total points at the bottom of the page.

_____ A mercy-giver possesses a tremendous capacity to love and to discern genuine love when exhibited by others.

_____ A mercy-giver focuses on the spiritual and emotional distress of others rather than his own physical distress.

_____ A mercy-giver attracts people who are hurting.

_____ A mercy-giver looks for opportunities to give preference to others.

_____ A mercy-giver postpones decisions and conflicts, except when eliminating great hurts.

_____ A mercy-giver needs deep friendships which exhibit mutual loyalty and commitment.

_____ A mercy-giver enjoys a special unity with those who are sensitive to the needs and feelings of others.

_____ A mercy-giver possesses an inner joy that can rejoice when others are blessed and weep when others are hurt.

_____ A mercy-giver relies on emotion rather than logic to guide him.

_____ A mercy-giver takes a stand when the cause is right.

_____ Total Points

Gifted for Life's Journey

Day Five

The Problems of the Gift of Mercy

The two personalities who experience the most friction in getting along are mercy and prophecy. The two disciples who were closest to Jesus were Peter and John. Luke 22:8 records that Jesus sent Peter and John together to prepare the Lord's Supper and the Passover. This arrangement could have caused problems, but they both relied on God to make their relationship work.

Sometimes, a mercy-giver can interfere in what God is trying to do in a person's life. She can be indecisive when she needs to be firm. She may transfer responsibilities to other people. But the greatest danger of being a person with the gift of mercy is that she can be misunderstood and find herself in a very precarious situation.

For example, if a young lady thinks she is in love with a boy and wants to please him, she can find herself engaged in a sexual relationship before she even realizes what is happening. Likewise, one of the employees in an office is having trouble in her marriage and has no one to confide in. The man at the desk next to hers has the gift of mercy, and so he naturally attracts those who are hurting. She begins to share her problems with him, and he offers his shoulder to her as solace. Before long, they are involved in an adulterous relationship.

The mercy-giver never intends for that to happen, but often he will find himself identifying with the other person and ignoring the conviction of the Holy Spirit, until he has gone too far and is trapped. Those of you who have this gift must establish safeguards to prevent this from ever happening.

Teenagers are especially susceptible to this. Don't let the other person misunderstand your expressions of love. Keep your relationships centered in Jesus Christ. As you exhibit your gift of mercy, don't get involved with anyone in an ungodly way. You don't need to come down to the same level of the person you are trying to help. Just because he is in the gutter, doesn't mean you have to crawl into the gutter with him in order to help him. It is your responsibility to show compassion by pulling him out of that situation.

The Gift of Mercy

The Practice of the Gift of Mercy

A Mercy-giver in the Spirit

Here are seven words to describe this gift when it is used in the Spirit.

Attentiveness

When a person with this gift is operating in the Spirit, he is keenly aware and attentive to the needs of others around him. His spiritual radar is up, and he can recognize others' needs.

Sensitivity

There is something special about a mercy-giver who is operating in the Spirit. He can see things others cannot see. He is very sensitive to the details of what is happening around him.

Fairness

People with the gift of mercy make great mediators, if they are in the Spirit and not in the flesh, because they have a tremendous sense of fairness. They will be fair to everyone involved in a conflict.

Compassion

They have a tremendous capacity to feel the suffering that others are experiencing.

Gentleness

All the edges of a mercy-giver's life are well-rounded. They have a wonderful capacity to gently, lovingly, and patiently meet the needs of others without being intrusive or interfering.

Meekness

They have a tremendous spirit of humility and are willing to suffer criticism to bring the other person through his painful situation.

Joy

As Romans 12:8 says, they will experience "hilarity" or overwhelming joy.

Gifted for Life's Journey

A Mercy-giver in the Flesh

There are seven words that describe the gift as it is abused when the person is operating in the flesh.

Disinterest

They don't care if someone is hurting. They are too focused on themselves and what they are experiencing in their own lives.

Callousness

Their soft touch is gone, and they are hardened. It is a sad thing to see a senior adult who has the gift of mercy, but has become embittered over the years. Perhaps he has been through some trials, and instead of being broken and becoming better, he has become bitter. That bitterness has caused his heart to become callused. There is a meanness, and cruelty, and anger about him, so that he can only think of himself. He has forgotten his God-given capacity to meet the needs of others.

Partiality

They will choose sides quickly and will not show fairness.

Apathy

They are uncaring about those who are hurting. It is so easy to slip into apathy. If you have the gift of mercy and find yourself not caring, be careful. Sin has invaded your life, and you are living in the flesh. This can happen when you unnecessarily take up a grievance for someone else. He may resolve his problem on his own, but as a mercy-giver, you carry that wound deeply. Rather than deal with it properly, you shield yourself by becoming apathetic. God then ceases to use you because you are operating in the flesh.

Rudeness

A mercy-giver in the flesh is like a bitter old prune—rude and uncaring about the feelings of others.

Anger

They can explode in volcanic anger, and they are impossible to live with.

112

The Gift of Mercy

Frustration

They experience frustration rather than joy because they're not properly using their God-given gift.

John's Example

The biblical example of the mercy-giver is John, who is called the beloved disciple throughout the scriptures. The Gospel of John speaks of love more than anything else. Legend has it that after his exile on the Isle of Patmos, John returned to Ephesus. At nearly 100 years of age, he would be carried into the church every Sunday to preach and would always have the same message: "Beloved, love one another." Love is the defining characteristic of the person with the gift of mercy.

Dealing With a Mercy-giver as a Child

If you have a son who has this gift, he will most likely be labeled as a sissy. He will be compassionate and will cry a lot. Many times the person with this gift is deeply wounded at a young age because children can be extremely cruel. Because of their childhood experiences, mercy-givers may develop defense mechanisms and facades to keep themselves from getting hurt. They think they can protect themselves by internalizing their hurts, when all they have really done is cause even more hurt.

Whatever our gift happens to be, we should all be grateful that we have a Savior who is merciful. Jesus is the epitome of all these gifts, including mercy. The worst situation I can imagine would be to stand before a God who had no mercy. Our God is merciful, and He cares intensely about our hurt and our pain.

He chose to enter our world to show us His mercy. That is why Isaiah 53:3 calls Jesus "a Man of sorrows and acquainted with grief." He knew how to hurt as we hurt. Hebrews 4:15 says, "For we do not have a High Priest who cannot sympathize with our weaknesses, but was in all points tempted as we are, yet without sin." He understands because he has experienced hurt as we have. He offers that mercy to you and to me. It is His gift of grace to us. It is by His mercy that you are saved and that you have the ability to know Him and walk with Him.

Gifted for Life's Journey

Your Scores

Take a few moments now to look back and copy your total score for each of the gifts. The gift in which you scored the highest is your primary gift.

_____ Prophesy

_____ Service

_____ Teaching

_____ Exhortation

_____ Giving

_____ Administration

_____ Mercy

My primary gift is _____.

My secondary gift is _____.

Week Nine

Living Your Gift

Day One

It is one thing to recognize your gift and understand how to use it within the church, but it is something else entirely to live with that gift on an everyday basis. We have studied the seven motivational gifts listed in Romans 12, and you have taken the tests to determine your gift. Some people don't score very high on any gift while others score high on several, and that's fine. It is the test on which you score the highest that indicates your gift. Now, we are going to learn how to live your gift, both in and out of the church.

I am always amazed at how God disperses the gifts throughout the church. He knows exactly what a church needs to function. All seven of these gifts together provide a complete picture of the Holy Spirit. Each of us is individually created to function as a part of the Body of Christ, and we each have an important role to fulfill in the church. Your gift is to be used in concert with all of the other gifts. The Holy Spirit called you to be a part of the Body of Christ, and if you are committed to Him, then you will want to be connected to His people.

Romans 12:4-6 expresses it this way: "For as we have many members in one body, but all the members do not have the same function, so we, being many, are one body in Christ, and individually members of one another. Having then gifts differing according to the grace that is given to us, let each exercise them accordingly." We are very different. We have different gifts and different places for service, and God has placed us within the body so that we can serve Him.

Once the Holy Spirit comes and resides within us, our gift becomes the channel through which God works in our lives to carry out His perfect will. As we allow God to work through us, we will not be frustrated in serving Him, and we won't feel as though we need to do everything. We can then concentrate on those things God has uniquely gifted us to do.

With that in mind, I want to look at three specific areas in which we can allow the Holy Spirit to work through our gift. These three areas will be helpful in using our gift in the real world where we live, work, and play.

Gifted for Life's Journey

Day Two

The Expression of the Gifts

The full expression of all seven of the gifts is best found in Jesus. The Bible tells us in Colossians 2:9, "For in Him dwells all the fullness of the Godhead bodily." In other words, He is the epitome of a prophet, a server, a teacher, an exhorter, a giver, an administrator, and a mercy-giver. Jesus is the only person who has ever possessed all seven gifts because, even though He is a man, He is also God.

Isaiah 11:1 says, "There shall come forth a Rod from the stem of Jesse and a Branch shall grow out of his roots." The word *stem* refers to a stump. In this verse the stem is Jesse, David's father. The words *Rod* and *Branch* both mean a twig or a fresh, green shoot, and refer to Jesus, who descended from the lineage of Jesse and David. In other words, out of the old, dead stump (Jesse and his descendants) sprang forth a fresh, new Branch (Jesus Christ), invigorated with life. Isaiah 11:2 goes on to give us a description of this Branch. "And the Spirit of the Lord will rest upon Him, the Spirit of wisdom and understanding, the Spirit of counsel and might, the Spirit of knowledge and of the fear of the Lord."

This verse is a very concise and accurate illustration of the seven gifts we have studied. If you want to see a perfect example of your gift in action, all you need to do is study the life of Jesus

First we see Him as the full embodiment of the prophet. In the Hebrew, "Spirit of the Lord" is literally *Ruach Yahweh.* Here, *Rauch* means the spirit communicating the will of God, and He exists for the sole purpose of carrying out God's will. This is the very essence of a prophet. He sees everything as either in or out of God's will with no gray areas in between.

It was Jesus' desire to stay in the center of God's will. In John 12:49, Jesus said, "For I have not spoken on My own authority; but the Father who sent Me gave Me a command, what I should say and what I should speak." Jesus was the perfect example of a prophet because he spoke with God's authority and carried out the will of His Father.

We also see that Jesus was the epitome of the server. The word *wisdom* in the Hebrew is *chocmah,* and it means to discern a situation based on experience. The server's primary means of operation is to analyze a situation so that practical needs can be met.

The Gift of Prophecy

That is what Jesus set about doing. Jesus often praised serving. In Mark 10:43(b) He says, "Whoever desires to become great among you shall be your servant." The great ones, Jesus said, will be servants.

Jesus was also the perfect teacher. The Hebrew word *binah* is translated *understanding,* and means the power to recognize the way things differ from a standard. The teacher evaluates a situation to see if it conforms to the standard of God's Word. We know that Jesus did that as He fulfilled the law in every single detail. Matthew 5:17 says, "Do not think that I came to destroy the Law or the Prophets. I did not come to destroy but to fulfill."

Jesus was also the prime example of an exhorter. The Hebrew word used for *counsel* is *etzah* which means the ability to form a right conclusion. Exhorters determine where people are spiritually, and then conclude where they need to be and how to get there. They can encourage them on to spiritual maturity. Jesus was constantly explaining the steps to victorious living. The "Sermon on the Mount" is one of the greatest exhortations on how to live a successful life. It is a powerful message from a powerful exhorter.

Jesus was also the ultimate example of a giver. The phrase, *Spirit of might,* is translated from the Hebrew word *geburah* and means the ability to carry out an established plan in a practical way. A giver is pragmatic and focused on whatever works. He will give his energy, time, talent, and money to benefit others, and to accomplish the plan of the gospel in a very practical way. He is willing to give whatever it takes.

John 15:13 says, "Greater love has no one than this, than to lay down one's life for his friends." Jesus gave His own life for you and me, and this makes Him the greatest giver of all.

He was also the ultimate administrator. Isaiah 11:2 continues with *the Spirit of knowledge.* In the Hebrew, the phrase means the Spirit of the knowledge of the Lord. It refers to the facts that one learns by experience and then communicates to others. An administrator organizes and leads others with the support of his experience. An administrator operates under and leads with authority.

Jesus himself operated under the authority of the Heavenly Father, and yet exercised all authority. Jesus said in Matthew 28:18, "All authority has been given to Me in heaven and on earth."

Jesus was also the best example of the mercy-giver. Isaiah 11:2 says that He had resting upon him "the fear of the Lord." The Hebrew word is *yirath Yahweh. Yahweh* is the Hebrew word for Lord and *yirath* is the word for fear. This is not the typical word meaning fear or reverence, but rather it means an awareness of one's own weakness that causes respect and reverence for the stronger one. That is a direct indication of what the mercy-giver is all about. He shows compassion and respect for those who are weak, and his compassion is intensified by his reverence for the Lord. Jesus often expressed compassion. John 11:35 tells us He wept at Lazarus' tomb. The Greek language indicates that He

Gifted for Life's Journey

was literally shaking as he walked toward the tomb. The same word is used to describe an earthquake. He was experiencing an emotional upheaval because of His compassion and love and His awareness of the needs of others.

Jesus spoke of the crowd following Him in Matthew 15:32, "I have compassion on the multitude because they have now continued with Me three days and have nothing to eat. And I do not want to send them away hungry, lest they faint on the way."

In summary, we see that Jesus Christ was the full expression of all seven gifts. We should look to Him for our role model, for He exemplifies each gift to its very highest degree. Whether you are a prophet, teacher, server, giver, administrator, mercy-giver, or exhorter, Jesus is your best example.

Day Three

The Exercise of the Gifts

Peter wrote to the believers in Rome, many of whom were about to face tremendous persecution, reminding them that they were uniquely gifted. In 1 Peter 4:10, he wrote, "As each one has received a gift, minister it to one another." We have learned that these personality gifts were given to us because we were created in the image of God. Although only Christians are energized by the presence of the Holy Spirit, every human being is given one of these seven gifts. It is an expression of the Spirit of God as He forms and molds the spirit of man. We receive this gift; we don't earn it. It is given to us by God, and reflects a portion of His character.

We are commanded by God to use our gift for the benefit of others. We are to serve one another using the talent God has given us. It is incorrect for anyone to say, "I can worship God just as well out in nature as I can in a church." Worship is not all personally directed and is not all about what benefits you. Worship also occurs when we use our gift to benefit and meet the needs of the Body of Christ.

1 Peter 4:10 continues, "…as good stewards of the manifold grace of God." The word *manifold* literally means multifaceted. We have looked at all seven facets of God's grace. He calls us to be good stewards of the grace that He bestows upon us. If you are gifted in more than one area, then you have a higher accountability regarding the way you use your gifts to benefit the body. One day

The Gift of Prophecy

you will stand before God and answer for the way in which you've used or misused your gift. Are you utilizing the giftedness that He has placed within you for the benefit of others?

In 1 Timothy 4:14, Paul advises Timothy, a young man in the ministry, "Do not neglect the gift that is in you, which was given to you by prophesy with the laying on of the hands of the eldership." The Greek word for *given* is *didomi*, which means to be brought forth or identified. Paul describes the time when someone with the gift of prophesy, along with the rest of the elders of the church, laid his hands on Timothy in a special ordination ceremony and identified his spiritual gift.

He goes on to say in 2 Timothy 1:6, "Therefore I remind you to stir up the gift of God which is in you through the laying on of my hands." Here we see that Paul himself had been involved in Timothy's ordination. The Greek word he used for *stir up* is *anazopureo*, which is in the present tense, and literally means to keep blazing. Paul is admonishing Timothy not to neglect his gift, but to use it to the glory of God and the benefit of His church.

Have you ever noticed how some Christians seem to be on fire for God? They have a passion that courses through their veins, and they give 100 percent of their energy to God. Then there are other Christians who never seem to fit. Every time they try to involve themselves in ministry, it's like trying to plug a square peg into a round hole. They just can't quite pull things together, and there is no sense of passion in their lives.

Paul is saying to Timothy that if you want to be an "on fire" Christian, then you must use the gift that God has given you. That is where your natural tendency of service lies, and that is how you can best be utilized to make a difference for God. Timothy was commanded not to neglect his gift, but to keep his life ablaze with the power of the Holy Spirit.

I encounter so many frustrated Christians trying their best to be on fire for God in an area in which they are not gifted. They really don't know how to light a fire in that area because they are like wet wood—heavy and useless.

We, as Christian leaders, have been guilty of squeezing others into molds where they really don't fit. When we need a Sunday school teacher or a person to serve on some committee, we corner the first person we see, and make them feel guilty until they finally agree to serve in that capacity; they may not even be gifted to serve in that particular area. It doesn't matter to us if they're out of their league, as long as we can say we filled the position.

Our goal and our desire should be to help people understand that God can use them in a unique capacity, but not to force them into a mold where God never intended for them to be. If we will be sensitive to the leadership of the Holy Spirit, every position that God wants to be filled in His Church will be filled. We must enlist people on the basis of God's wisdom and as He leads. The Church is the Body of Christ, and we should allow Him to place people where He wants them.

Gifted for Life's Journey

You don't have to do everything in the church, serve on every committee, and teach every class. In fact, if you are neglecting your family to occupy a position in your church, then you are in sin. Your primary responsibility is to minister to your family and to be a godly example to them. You can do that only if you are operating on the basis of the gift God has given you.

There are people in the church who are so uniquely gifted that they could do things I could never dream of doing. God puts us together in the same church so that we can work together as a team to accomplish His will. As we then combine the fires that are ablaze within us, God lights a fire in other hearts because they, too, are doing what they are gifted to do.

In 1 Corinthians 12:7, we read, "But the manifestation of the Spirit is given to each one for the profit of all." The word for *manifestation* in the Greek is the word *phaneroosis,* and it is taken from a word that means a lamp or lantern. We could say, "The lantern of the Spirit is given to each one for the profit of all." When we let the Spirit shine through us, we touch one another's lives as we serve the Lord out of an overflow of joy and a God-given sense of fulfillment.

Others will begin to notice that there is a depth in our lives that has never been there before. We have tapped into a channel through which God's grace naturally flows through our lives, just as water follows the path of least resistance and flows downhill. As that path of our particular spiritual gift becomes the path through which God's grace shines in our lives, we begin to look at our entire life and our circumstances through our gifts.

Day Four

There are three specific areas where your gifts can and should have an impact.

Your Career

Statistics show us that two out of three people are dissatisfied with their present job. Many people waste years working in an area that fails to use the gift that God has given them.

Each gift is oriented toward certain careers. The prophet, for example, functions well in high pressure situations. He is ideally suited for careers such as air traffic controller or law enforcement officer. He also thrives in the military, the mission field, the ministry, the medical profession, or the teaching profession.

The server is a hands-on person. He wants to work in an area that is more pragmatic, and he doesn't like pressure. He works well as an accountant, a farmer, an architect, an assembly line worker, a bank teller, a barber or beautician, construction worker, firefighter, secretary, vocational teacher, truck driver, or landscaper.

The teacher is more research oriented. He needs a vocation that will require a great deal of study such as an archeologist, a scientist, professor, computer programmer, engineer, doctor, journalist, surgeon, math or science teacher, writer, market analyst, pharmacist, or psychiatrist.

The exhorter is more practical and self-help oriented. He loves to be involved in anything in which he can see a project come to completion fairly rapidly. Vocations such as advertising agent, guidance counselor, occupational therapist, politician, psychologist, recreation leader, social worker, or travel agent fit him. Some of the best teachers that you remember from your childhood were probably exhorters because they could gently lead you from where you were to where you needed to be.

Givers are some of the most well rounded people. They love to give of themselves in almost any capacity imaginable. They make good actors, auditors, auctioneers, bankers, business consultants, buyers, contractors, economists, and salesmen. A giver makes a good evangelist because he loves to give away the greatest gift of all, the gift of eternal life.

Administrators are more management oriented; they want to be in leadership positions. They manage homes or businesses well. They are good personnel managers, media producers, hospital or school administrators, teachers, store managers, or business owners.

The mercy-givers are more creative. They make good artists, child care providers, interior decorators, florists, musicians, photographers, physical therapists, elementary school teachers, or veterinarians.

This list is extremely broad, and God may not have you in one of the fields in which you are gifted. If you are fulfilled in your job, but you are not working in an area that befits your giftedness, then that is fine. It may be that God has you in that particular area so that you can be strengthened or enhanced in another area; He may also be maturing you. The important thing for you to know is that God has you where He wants you and that you know you are in God's will.

Your Counseling

This is how you relate to others. Knowing someone's spiritual gift will help you relate to him. If you learn what a person's gift is, it will help you in your marriage or raising your children. If you know for example that you are a prophet and you have a mercy-giver for a child, you will not have to use corporal punishment on your child very often. All you need to do is speak firmly, which prophets tend to do naturally, and that child will be corrected.

You also know that, if you are a mercy-giver and you have a prophet for a child, it will be hard for you to discipline him. You will go to pieces every time you have to spank him, and he will hardly be affected by the punishment. So, as a mercy-giver, you must alter your discipline to insure that your child is properly controlled.

Another time when it is helpful to understand spiritual gifts, is when witnessing to someone. If you can observe what a person's personality is, you can determine the best way to reach him. For example, a prophet will respond best to questions about right and wrong. He loves to talk about issues such as good versus evil, God's justice, and why bad things happen to good people. He wants to get down to the basics of life. You should prepare in advance by studying these issues and being ready with answers to his questions.

A server wants a faith that is practical and useful. He responds best to questions like, "What is man's greatest need?" or, "Do you think good works will help a person get to heaven?" These issues will arouse interest in a server, and you should able to provide answers. The teacher, on the other hand, wants facts. He wants to know the basis or proof for what you share. Books like Josh McDowell's *Evidence That Demands a Verdict* are useful in witnessing to a teacher. The teacher responds well to being shown proof, not just told what you believe.

The exhorter is concerned with people's problems and what he can do to help. He responds well to questions like, "What are the best ways to help people overcome their problems?" or, "What do you consider most important for a fulfilled life?" Those questions energize an exhorter and cause him to want to respond.

A giver has a naturally eager response to the gospel. I love to lead a giver to Jesus; he is the quickest because he loves to give and to have something worth giving. Often, just a simple presentation of the gospel can lead a giver to Jesus Christ.

An administrator is interested in the overall view of life and the universe. He wants answers to deep questions like, "Why do you think God created man?"

Mercy-givers relate to the feelings of others. If you want to witness to a mercy-giver, you can ask him, "How do you feel God wants us to treat each other?" or, "Do you feel there is any hope for the suffering people of the world?" Questions like this engage their emotions and cause them to respond to the gospel.

As you study these gifts, you will better understand how to relate to people, whether it is your children, your spouse, or someone to whom you are witnessing.

The Gift of Prophecy

Your Church

Jesus is the full expression of all the gifts, and the Church, as the Body of Christ, is His expression of the gifts to the world. That is why it is so important for us to work together as Christians. We have a responsibility to the world to be the kind of example that Jesus wants us to be, so we can fulfill the ministry to which we are called.

Everyone is going to perform his ministry differently, but we are all called to minister. Each one of us has a gift, and we can all be a witness to others. There may be someone you, as a mercy-giver, can reach. But I can't reach them. That's great because God will use us all, wherever we are needed.

Here is an example of how the different gifts are used to carry out the ministry of the church. Seven people, each with a different gift, might respond differently to a person who is confined to bed with a long-term illness.

- The prophet will pray both privately and at the bedside for healing, strength, and endurance because he realizes God is doing a work in the person's life.

- The server will bring meals to her family, offer to do housework, run errands, and mow her lawn.

- The teacher will, at first, have a difficult time relating to the person. He will eventually bring some good books for the patient to read. Because he knows these things would help him, he assumes it will help the patient, as well.

- The exhorter will go immediately to cheer the patient up, and he will assure her that she will soon be feeling better.

- The giver will bring food and other gifts, and spend time talking with the sick person.

- The administrator will find out what she needs and then organize the church to meet those needs. He will arrange for her Sunday school class to bring meals, and that everything is done to take care of her.

- The mercy-giver will ask how she feels, empathize, hug, weep, and stay by her bedside. She will do all she can to care for the patient.

Every one of those seven people can meet a different need in the life of that patient. Each one can minister to a need that Jesus would meet. When you

Gifted for Life's Journey

combine all seven expressions of concern, you see what Jesus would do for her because He is the expression of all seven gifts. That is why we need each other; we must work in concert to carry out effective ministries.

In small groups, more than any other place in the life of the church, you can use your gift in ministry. A prophet would probably want to teach the older youth or adult classes. A server would prefer to assist the teacher, possibly as a secretary, or perhaps work in the nursery. A teacher would prefer to teach adults and college students, or classes that deal with a specific topic. An exhorter would be happy to teach any age, but may be especially good with teenagers and children. A giver would do well teaching any age, and may also want to help promote mission offerings or contributions. An administrator would be delighted to be in charge—to be a department superintendent, or teach an adult class. And a mercy-giver would love to work with children's, pre-school, or nursery departments.

God made you unique. Don't plug yourself into a square hole if you are a round peg; you will not fit. Be what God wants you to be. There is no need to be frustrated when God can so naturally fit you where He wants you to serve.

I heard a story about a group of animals who wanted to do something about the problems of the world, so they decided to organize a school. They adopted a curriculum consisting of running, climbing, swimming, and flying, and declared that every animal must take all of the courses.

The duck was excellent in swimming, but he made only passing grades in flying, and was poor in running. Since he was such a slow runner, he had to stay after school to practice running. This caused his webbed feet to become badly worn, which made him only average at swimming. No one really worried about this except the duck, who became extremely frustrated.

The rabbit started off at the top of his class in running, but soon developed a nervous twitch in his leg because of so much make-up work in swimming. The twitch slowed him down and made him a so-so runner.

The squirrel was excellent in climbing; but he was frustrated in flying class because the teacher made him start from the ground instead of from the treetop. He developed cramps in his legs from trying to run fast enough to leap from the ground to fly, so he only made a "C" in climbing and a "D" in running.

The eagle, on the other hand, was a problem student. He was severely disciplined for being a nonconformist. In climbing class he beat the other animals to the top of the tree but insisted on getting there his own way—by flying.

We know rabbits don't fly, and eagles don't swim. Ducks look ridiculous trying to climb, and squirrels don't have feathers. God gave them unique capacities, and He has made you unique, too. You can find yourself frustrated because you are serving God out of a sense of obligation. If you are doing that, stop it! Begin serving God because you love what you are doing, and allow Him to use you to make a difference.

The Gift of Prophecy

Day Five

The Experience of the Gifts

How do we keep our gift blazing so that we are a light shining in the darkness to bring others to Jesus? The key is found in 2 Corinthians 3:18, which says, "But we all, with unveiled face beholding as in a mirror the glory of the Lord, are being transformed into the same image from glory to glory, just as by the Spirit of the Lord."

The first requirement is to get rid of the sin that acts as a veil—or a barrier—between you and the Lord, and keeps you from being an effective light for Him. Secondly, you must keep your focus on Jesus and His example, and allow the glory of the Lord to be reflected from you, just as light is from a mirror. Next, you will be changed—or transformed—becoming more like Jesus in the process. Finally, recognize that it is Jesus, or "the Spirit of the Lord," who transforms you, with all seven facets of His presence.

Each of us has a primary gift, and we should be growing and maturing in all the others. This happens when we are transformed daily into the image of Christ, who is the complete expression of all seven gifts.

We read in 1 John 3:2, "Beloved, now we are children of God; and it has not yet been revealed what we shall be, but we know that when He is revealed, we shall be like Him, for we shall see Him as He is." In other words, the more we mature, the more we become like Jesus. Right now, we cannot even comprehend what we will become, but we will be like Him when we are received into the glory that He has in store for us.

There are four ways to continue in the process of maturing. First, confess all known sin. Second, surrender every area of your life as it is revealed by the Holy Spirit. Third, serve in the area of your gift. Blaze for the Lord! Fourth, grow in those areas where you are weak by practicing them, even though doing so will feel unnatural to you. As you grow, you become more merciful, more prophetic, more giving, and ultimately, more like Jesus

As you practice these four steps, a drastic change will take place in your life. No longer will you be conformed to this world, according to Romans 12:2, but that you will be transformed by the renewing of your mind. In the process of sanctification, or being set aside for the Lord, you will be moving from glory to glory. What a beautiful picture this is of God's amazing love for us!